GIRL GROUPS

PIANO • V

ISBN 0-634-01699-7

HAL•LEONARD®
CORPORATION

7777 W. Bluemound Rd. P.O. Box 13819 Milwaukee, WI 53213

Visit Hal Leonard Online at
www.halleonard.com

CONTENTS

ALPHABETICALLY BY GROUP

CONTENTS

ALPHABETICALLY BY SONG TITLE

GIRL GROUPS

A Rock and Roll Tradition

By Elaine Schmidt

There are two versions of the story behind the birth of the first rock era girl groups. In one version, four teenage girls from the Saint Anthony of Padua school in the Bronx hang out backstage after a taping of the Alan Freed Show, hoping to meet their idol, Frankie Lymon. They begin singing, something they had been doing together for a while, just to pass the time. Songwriter/record producer Richard Barrett chances to hear them and eventually convinces George Goldner, owner of Rama records, to give the girls a shot. In the other version of the story, the girls still hang around the theater, but they are there for no other reason than to catch Barrett's ear. Whichever version of the story is true, the result is the same. The girls were outside the theater and Barrett heard them singing. He worked with them for several months until he felt they were ready to make their debut recording. The girls scored a few local hits, and then in 1959 they made it to number 15 on the pop charts with the song "Maybe." The girls, who had named themselves the Chantels, were the first of what would become a flood of all-girl singing groups, most of them teenage high schoolers, that would score hit after hit during the late '50s and early '60s, blurring the lines between pop, rock and R&B.

The timing of the girl groups' arrival was not coincidental. Rock and roll was in trouble by the late '50s and new blood was needed. Elvis' hips had horrified a generation of American parents. Fears that rock and roll would corrupt America's youth were seemingly confirmed with such events as Jerry Lee Lewis' marriage to his fourteen-year-old cousin. The youth, too, were disillusioned. Buddy Holly and Ritchie Valens were dead, and federal investigations into payola in the rock and roll industry were just getting underway. If the industry was going to survive, something had to change. Just as the scrubbed faces and spotless images of Pat Boone, Frankie Avalon and Bobby Rydell were a calculated marketing tool, so were the fresh faces and angelic sounds of the early girl groups. Female vocal ensembles were nothing new to popular music. Female blues duets had their heyday in the 1920s. The Andrews Sisters and the Dinning Sisters had made their mark in the '40s. Other sister acts, and faux sister acts, continued the pop tradition in the early '50s. But the girl groups of the '50s and '60s were a different story. For one thing, they were practically children, and for another, they were part of the rock and R&B worlds.

Girl groups, as they quickly became known, were largely teenagers singing to teenagers about the things that mattered to teenagers. Most of their songs dealt with such topics as true love, unrequited love, strife with parents, school, and loving the wrong boy. Although the sound of these groups has been described as part doo-wop and part R&B, it was more than that. Their style was part barbershop, part church choir and part rock and roll. And it was something else. It was innocent. The voices of girls singing in close harmony had a compelling sweetness that audiences found irresistible. Most of the girl singers were African-American at a time when racial segregation kept performers of color off mainstream television. Although they could not appear on programs such as "The Ed Sullivan Show" (a taboo the Supremes later broke), the girl groups scored hit after hit both in the U.S. and abroad. Most of the groups charted on both the pop and R&B charts, garnering a wide crossover audience.

If issues of race limited opportunities for the girl groups at first, issues of gender and age compounded their difficulties. Not only were female performers simply not taken seriously in the music business, these really were just girls. The young girls were part of musical machinery that sent the likes of producers/record company owners Phil Spector and Berry Gordy Jr. to the bank, while giving little back to the girls themselves. Many of the groups received little money for their work, leading to numerous lawsuits and much bitterness years later. Most of the girl groups did not write their own songs, nor did they have much say over what they would record. For some of the groups, individual members were completely expendable. A group's name might appear on several different records, but each one would have been recorded by a different band of singers. Teen magazines carried on at great length about the male pop and rock stars of the day, those boys groomed for teen consumption, but they largely ignored the girl groups.

For Berry Gordy Jr., owner of Motown Records, and songwriter/producer Smokey Robinson, the girl groups were pay dirt. The Marvelettes' recording of "Please Mr. Postman" was the first record from the then struggling label to hit number 1 on the charts. Capitalizing on what had worked once, Gordy quickly recorded another girl group, Martha & The Vandellas. The group had been singing backup vocals for Motown when Gordy recorded them singing "Come Get These Memories." "Heatwave" and "Dancing in the Street" soon followed, cementing Gordy's girl group formula. Motown became the source of many of the girl groups' hits over the next few years. It also became something of a "performer factory." Gordy hired Maxine Powell, who had run a finishing and modeling school, and choreographer Cholly Adams to create a sort of prep school for aspiring acts. As the groups were being primed in the arts of poise, polish and grace, Maurice King was hired to teach the skill of on-stage patter. By the mid 1960s, the Motown machine could take poor, inner-city Detroit kids and turn them into poised performers, creating the unmistakable image of the Motown artists.

The other producer to reap a fortune from the girl group sound was Phil Spector. A millionaire by age twenty-one, the young Spector's talents included song writing, singing, guitar playing and a remarkable flair for producing. Establishing his own record label, Philles, and producing such records as the Crystals' "There's No Other (Like My Baby)," "Da Doo Ron Ron" and "Uptown," Spector created what came to be known as the Wall of Sound. The Wall was a thick background of instrumentals and vocals created through careful over-dubbing. In 1964 he was referred to as the "the first tycoon of teen."

By the mid 1960s, the rock scene was changing yet again. The British had arrived and were pushing the girl groups off the charts. Although some of the groups toured with the British acts for a time, their sound was soon seen as too sweet and out of style. By the time the Rolling Stones, the self-proclaimed bad boys of rock, arrived, the girl group era was gasping its last breath. Some of the groups managed to hold on, playing rock revival shows and taking local gigs. Some of them held on by altering their style and sound to fit the changing times. The Supremes were the anomaly of the era. Their sophisticated image and satin sound had given them a unique niche from the start; they were Motown's hottest property. This class act not only survived the British invasion, but also thrived in its wake. However, the onslaught of British lads into American rock made one thing certain: the days of white-gloved schoolgirls crooning cotton candy hits were over.

The golden age of girl groups in rock music may have faded with the British invasion, but the point had been made: all-female bands could make hits. One of the greatest achievements of the scores of young girls who filled the airwaves with songs for those few years was to give women a place in rock and roll. Women had successfully performed and recorded jazz and blues for decades before the rock and roll girl groups appeared. But since its arrival on the national scene in 1954, rock had remained a male domain. Bill Haley, Elvis Presley, Buddy Holly, the Big Bopper, Ritchie Valens and scores of other men sang rock and roll to and about women. But for the most part, women did not find a voice in rock and roll until the girl groups appeared.

In the years since the Chantels first crooned for Richard Barrett, women have become powerful forces in the world of rock music. Although their goals were often as small as getting just one record on the air, the girls group of the late '50s and early '60s made profound changes in the way the industry dealt with women, gradually breaking down both gender and racial barriers. They paved the way for groups like Sister Sledge and the Spice Girls that would follow, and also for solo artists like Janis Joplin, Madonna and countless others.

Although much of the pop and R&B of its era has a dated, simplistic feel to it, the best of the girl group recordings are as fresh forty years after their release as when new. In trying to create a unique sound, one that was not based on sheer power, rebellion and rhythmic drive, the girl groups and their managers created some of the most carefully crafted, enduring and upbeat music of the early rock era. At any given time, somewhere in the world, someone is sure to always be singing along with the Supremes.

THE
GROUPS

THE ANGELS

One of the most successful of the early '60s girl groups, the Angels hit number 1 with "My Boyfriend's Back" (1963). The Angels' roots go back to the Starlets, a short-lived group from Orange, New Jersey which included sisters Barbara and Phyllis "Jiggs" Allbut. When the sisters began singing backup vocals with Linda Jansen in New York, a new group was born. The girls called themselves the Blue Angels, literally drawing the name from a hat. With the name shortened to the Angels, the group hit number 14 on the pop charts with their debut single "Till" (1961). Jansen left the group in 1962, replaced by Peggy Santiglia. Although they never came up with another hit like "My Boyfriend's Back," the group toured the U.S. and Europe in 1964 and continued to record through 1968. They recorded backup vocals for a number of artists and were heard in numerous commercials until they disbanded in 1969. The Angels reunited in the early '70s, cutting another single in 1974.

B*WITCHED

These four Dublin girls hit number 1 on the UK pop charts in 1998 with the single "C'est La Vie." They are the youngest girl group ever to hit that top spot. They continued breaking records by sending their next four singles straight to number 1. Members Lindsay Armaou, Sinead O'Carroll and twin sisters Keavy and Edele Lynch (whose brother Shane is a member of Boyzone) have been described as the first Irish hip-hop act. After "C'est La Vie" took Europe by storm, the song hit the Top Ten in the U.S.

THE BANGLES

Starting out in 1981 as the Colours, guitarist/vocalist Susanna Hoffs, drummer/vocalist Debbi Peterson, guitarist/vocalist Vicki Peterson and bassist/vocalist Annette Zilinskas (replaced by Michelle Steele in 1983) were formed by a newspaper ad looking for band members. The Colours changed its name to the Supersonic Bangs, later shortening it to the Bangs. When they discovered that another group had been using that name, they modified it to the Bangles. Although they started out with intentions of sharing song writing and lead vocals, media attention quickly focused on Hoffs. After a string of hits such as "Manic Monday," "Eternal Flame" and "Walk Like an Egyptian," resentment over Hoffs' spot in the limelight broke up the band in 1989.

THE CHIFFONS

Vocalists Barbara Lee, Patricia Bennett and Judy Craig met at their Bronx high school and began singing together. Literally picking their name out of a hat, the girls recorded a cover of the Shirelles' "Tonight's the Night" in 1960, none of them yet fifteen years old. Although the record charted, the Chiffons largely disappeared until 1962, when Sylvia Peterson joined to make it a quartet. The group had a three-year run of hits, including "One Fine Day" (1963) and "Sweet Talkin' Guy" (1966). At the same time as the Chiffons were on the charts with "One Fine Day," they recorded several songs on a subsidiary label under the name the Four Pennies. They charted as the Pennies, although never reaching very high. In 1975, in response to George Harrison's unintentional plagiarization of their hit "He's So Fine," the group recorded Harrison's version of "My Sweet Lord." The Chiffons continued to perform locally, without Judy Craig, into the '80s.

THE CHORDETTES

The Chordettes were an anomaly in the mid 1950s. The rock and roll era girl group sound had not yet been identified or cultivated when "Mister Sandman," their second single, went straight to the top of the charts. They began as a folksy barbershop ensemble in Sheboygan, Wisconsin in the late '40s, with singers Dorothy Schwartz, Jinny Lockard, Carol Buschman and Janet Ertel. They first appeared on Arthur Godfrey's "Talent Scouts" radio show in 1949; the show soon moved to television. In 1953 Dorothy was replaced by Lynn Evans and Jinny was replaced by Margie Needham. The Chordettes survived the 1954 dawn of rock and roll at first by recording songs that managed to appeal to both adults and teens, and later by recording covers of popular tunes. In 1958 they hit the number 2 spot with "Lollipop." But the end was near. They were simply not "cool" enough to compete with younger talent, scoring their last hit in 1961.

THE COOKIES

Original Cookies members Margie Hendrix, Ethel "Earl-Jean" McCrea and Pat Lyles had their first Top Ten R&B hit in 1956. The group was heard backing songs for Joe Turner and Chuck Willis before they became Ray Charles' Raelettes for a time. In 1962 the Cookies reappeared, with McCrea being the only holdover from the original cast. In addition to singing backup vocals for Neil Sedaka, Little Eva and Carole King, the group had a hit of their own with "Chains" in 1963, a song covered by none other than the Beatles. The Cookies recorded for the last time in 1967.

THE CRYSTALS

Formed in 1961, the Crystals were schoolgirls from Brooklyn. Dee Dee Kennibrew, Dolores "La La" Brooks, Mary Thomas, Barbara Alston and Patricia Wright formed the group that helped hone Phil Spector's Wall of Sound style. Spector, who had just started the Philles label, backed the girls' voices with thick tracks of instrumentals and vocals. The fact that he was more interested in a sound than in the group is evidenced by the fact that the group's only number 1 hit, "Da Doo Ron Ron," was actually recorded under the Crystals' name by some L.A. session singers known as the Blossoms. The Crystals had several hits, including "Uptown" and "He's Sure the Boy I Love," both in 1962. Mary Thomas left to get married in 1962, but the girls continued as a quartet. They had tremendous success overseas, touring with Johnny Mathis, Jackie Wilson and James Brown. Although the group disbanded in 1967, Dee Dee brought La La, Barbara and Mary back together in 1971 for a rock revival show. Barbara, Mary and Dee Dee worked together until Barbara left in 1973. Dee Dee carried on with Darlene Davis and Marilyn Byers. In 1986 the Crystals, now La La, Dee Dee, Darlene and Gretchen Gale-Prendatt, recorded an album entitled *The Crystals: He's a Rebel.*

DESTINY'S CHILD

Like most of the girl groups of the '50s and '60s, the four singers of Destiny's Child came together as schoolgirls. The difference was that they brought their schoolgirl act to fame in the 1990s. The Texas-based quartet of best friends Beyoncé, Kelly, LaTavia and Le Toya appeared on "Star Search" in 1992, aged nine and ten at the time. Their song "Bills, Bills, Bills," from the album *The Writing's on the Wall*, is a no-holds barred, funny look at boyfriends whose images tarnish with time.

DIXIE CHICKS

A few Dallas schoolgirls decided to take their little musical act to the street corners in 1989 to play for passers-by. Folks liked what they heard and asked the girls what their band was called. After a few weeks of going nameless, the girls took the name Dixie Chicken from a Little Feat song. It quickly became Dixie Chicks. Although they started out on the street corner with a few more players, the group is now a vocal trio that plays guitar, mandolin, dobro, banjo and fiddle. Members Natalie Maines, Emily Erwin and Martie Seidel won their first Country Music Association Award in 1998. They received three Grammy nominations in 1999, winning in the categories of Best Country Performance by a Duo or Group with Vocal ("Ready to Run," heard in the film *Runaway Bride*) and Best Country Album (*Fly*). At this writing, the Dixie Chicks are making the big stretch to cross over to the pop charts.

EN VOGUE

Vocalists Cindy Herron, Maxine Jones, Terry Ellis and Dawn Robinson, better known as the group Vogue, came together in 1988 when San Francisco Bay area producers Thomas Elroy and Denzil Foster held auditions for an R&B girl group. Vogue added two songs to the concept album *FM2*. After altering its name, the group recorded several hits. Part of their appeal is the democratic way in which they share the limelight, trading off lead vocals. Their image was cultivated chic, complete with designer costumes. The girls' first album, *Born to Sing*, included a reworked version of the Andrews Sisters' "Boogie Woogie Bugle Boy," entitled "Hip Hop Bugle Boy." They released their first single, "Hold On," in 1990. It went to number 1 on the R&B chart and number 2 on the pop chart.

THE GO-GO'S

Formed in Hollywood in 1978 as the Misfits, the Go-Go's became the most popular all-girl band of the late '70s and early '80s. Although the group came out of the California punk scene, their hits, "We Got the Beat," "Vacation" and others had a high energy, new wave pop sound. The original members, Belinda Carlisle on vocals, Jane Wiedlin on guitar and vocals, Charlotte Caffey on lead guitar and vocals, Margot Olaverra on bass and Elissa Bello on drums, started out in California parties and clubs. In 1979 drummer Elissa Bello was replaced by Gina Schock. The group's first success came in England, where they toured during half of 1980. Although an import copy of "We Got the Beat" became an underground hit in the U.S., they had a tough time landing a record contract in the States. Late in 1980 bassist Olaverra was replaced by Kathy Valentine. In 1981 they signed an American record contract and a re-recorded version of "We Got the Beat" went to number 2 on the charts. The group split up in 1985, reuniting briefly in 1990. Caffey created a new group in 1989 called the Graces. The Go-Go's reunited once again in 1994. Belinda Carlisle, with her California blonde good looks, attained a fame of her own equaling that of the Go-Go's.

INDIGO GIRLS

Decidedly more women than girls, the Indigo Girls (two childhood friends from Decatur, Georgia) formed the band Saliers & Ray in 1980. By 1983 Emily Saliers and Amy Ray, both guitarist/vocalists, had changed their name to the Indigo Girls. Their voices and styles are a study in contrasts that balance. Ray is an alto-voiced rocker while Saliers is a soprano with a folk bent. After developing a following via a couple of independent releases, the pair signed with the Epic label. The following they had developed gave them the clout to retain artistic freedom in their record deal. Throughout their career, the two singers have devoted both time and money to issues that matter to them. They often sing about such topics as women's rights, protection of the environment and the rights of indigenous peoples. They are known for their benefit concerts on behalf of the Children's Health Fund and Habitat for Humanity.

THE JUDDS

The Judds, mother Naomi and daughter Wynonna, took their old-fashioned tunes and seamlessly blended voices to the top of the country and western charts in the mid 1980s. They remained the most beloved mother-daughter act in music until Naomi's chronic hepatitis forced her to retire in 1991. The pair charted with such hits as "Mama He's Crazy" (1984), "A Girl's Night Out" (1985) and "Rockin' with the Rhythm of the Rain" (1986), winning five Grammys for Best Country Vocal Duet. A highly emotional farewell tour during 1991 meant the beginning of Wynonna's solo efforts, which drew critical acclaim. With Naomi's disease in remission, the pair reunited for a nationally televised Super Bowl performance in 1994. Naomi published her memoirs, *Love Can Build a Bridge*, in 1995.

LABELLE

Formed as Patti LaBelle & The Blue Belles in 1961, LaBelle grew from a standard-issue girl group into a funky, space-queen band of politically conscious rock divas. The group consisted of vocalists Patti LaBelle (born Patricia Louise Holt), Nona Hendryx, Sarah Dash and Cindy Birdsong. Birdsong left in 1967 to replace Florence Ballard in the Supremes. The group was floundering, though still playing the Apollo Theatre, when new management updated their image and breathed life into the act. In 1974 they became the first black group ever to play the Metropolitan Opera House, where they debuted their only million-selling hit, "Lady Marmalade." The group broke up in 1976 and Patti went on to a solo career. They reunited in 1991 to record "Release Yourself" on Patti LaBelle's solo album *Burnin'*.

MARTHA & THE VANDELLAS

Martha Reeves sang in a group called the Del-Phis while in high school. Her group members included Annette Beard and Rosalind Ashford. The group cut one record while still in high school and Martha did a little solo work as well. Eventually the girls were called in to record backup vocals for a Marvin Gaye song. They named themselves the Vandellas and began cutting records of their own. With an earthier, more soul-oriented sound than many of their Motown counterparts, they scored several timeless hits, including "Heatwave" (1963), "Dancing in the Street" (1964) and "Nowhere to Run" (1965). In 1967 their name changed to Martha & The Vandellas. Beard had retired in 1963 and was replaced by Betty Kelly, formerly of the Velvettes. Kelly left in 1967, replaced by Lois Reeves, Martha's younger sister. Ashford left in 1969, succeeded by Sandra Tilley, another former Velvette. The group disbanded in 1973, but Martha continued to record as a soloist, performing on special occasions with Beard and Ashford.

THE MARVELETTES

When five seventeen-year-old girls from Inkster, Michigan sang a couple of songs for Motown's Berry Gordy Jr. and Smokey Robinson, they were hoping for instant stardom. Gordy and Robinson were interested, but sent the girls home to come up with something original. When they came back with "Please Mr. Postman," rewritten by one of the group's members, the Marvelettes were in the door at magical Motown. Vocalists Gladys Horton, Katherine Anderson, Georgeanna Tillman (Georgie Dobbins), Juanita Cowart and Wanda Young, with their name changed from the Marvels to the Marvelettes, had not only their

THE MARVELETTES

first single with the song, but they also had Motown's first number 1 hit on the pop charts. The song stayed on the charts for nearly six months. Juanita left the group in 1965, followed soon after by Georgeanna. Eventually Gladys left as well, replaced by Anne Bogan. When Motown moved to L.A. in 1969, Wanda decided to stay in Detroit, putting an end to the group, although more singles were issued over the next two years.

THE McGUIRE SISTERS

Like the Chordettes, the McGuire Sisters were singing and recording long before girl groups became a fad. The McGuires, Phyllis, Dorothy and Christine, began singing together as children in Middletown, Ohio during the 1930s. Their career began in the church where their father was a minister, where they were in great demand for picnics, weddings and services. By 1949 they were singing pop, and by 1950 they were touring for the USO. Like the Chordettes, they appeared on Arthur Godfrey's "Talent Scouts." They soon replaced the Chordettes, singing on his morning show for some six years, becoming one of the most well-known vocal groups in the country. In 1954 they charted with "Pine Tree, Pine Over Me" and "Goodnight Sweetheart, Goodnight." In 1955 they hit number 1 with "Sincerely." They commanded the highest advertising fee up to that time when they recorded commercials for Coca-Cola. When the group stopped recording in the mid 1960s, lead singer Phyllis established a solo career. They reunited in 1985, and in 1989 they performed at President George Bush's inauguration.

THE POINTER SISTERS

Ruth, Anita, Bonnie and June Pointer grew up on gospel music in Oakland, California. Priding themselves on a wide repertoire of styles, the sisters were singing backups for the likes of Chicago, Grace Slick and Boz Scaggs in the early '70s when they were heard and signed by the Atlantic label. When they began releasing their own records in 1971, they wanted to avoid comparisons to the Supremes, so they wore vivid, '40s-style costumes, which brought a comparison to the Andrews Sisters instead. June's nervous breakdown and Bonnie's decision to go solo gave the group a few fallow years, but in the late '70s Ruth, Anita and June were back on the charts as a trio. They hit number 3 on the pop charts and number 10 on the R&B charts in 1980 with "He's So Shy." In 1982 they got back on the charts with their definitive single, "I'm So Excited," which hit number 9 on the pop charts with a remix of the song in 1984. The group's last hit was "Be There" (1987), from the film *Beverly Hills Cop II*.

THE SHANGRI-LAS

Identical twins Mary Ann and Marge Ganser and their good friends, sisters Liz and Mary Weiss, formed one of the few white girl groups of the genre's golden age. Their songs were largely musical melodramas written for them by songwriter/producer George "Shadow" Morton. The girls' demo recording was as much an audition for Morton as it was for the group. In 1964, with a young Billy Joel on piano, they recorded Morton's "Remember (Walking in the Sand)." The song eventually hit number 14 on the pop charts, followed by the group's most memorable melodrama, "Leader of the Pack." That bad girl anthem went straight to number 1, initiating the practice of killing off characters in their lyrics. By the end of 1964, the British invasion was in full swing, but the girls remained on the charts. Eventually they would even perform with the Beatles. But their days were numbered. Liz had left early on, turning the group into a trio. By the late '60s the Shangri-Las disbanded. Mary Ann died in 1971. In 1989 the three surviving singers turned up at the Palisades Amusement Park Reunion Concert at the Meadowlands Arena in New Jersey. After singing a few of their hits, the group roared on-stage on motorcycles and brought the house down with "Leader of the Pack."

THE SHIRELLES

In the midst of an era of manufactured girl groups who were handed the repertoire they were to perform, the Shirelles were one of the few groups to write some of their own hits. Vocalists Shirley Owens, Addie "Mickey" Harris, Doris Coley and Beverly Lee came together in 1957 in Passaic, New Jersey. Originally calling themselves the Poquellos (birds), the group went on to become the most popular of the early '60s girl groups. When friend Mary Jane Greenberg heard them sing, their fortunes changed. Mary Jane asked if they would sing for her mother, Florence Greenberg, who owned Tiara Records at the time. The girls declined repeatedly before finally agreeing to audition in Florence's living room. Florence changed the group's name and put together a single for them. The Shirelles first hit the charts in 1959. When they were presented with a Carole King/Gerry Goffin song entitled "Tomorrow" in 1960, they disliked it and had to be pressured into recording it. It was released that fall as the great "Will You Still Love Me Tomorrow," which took them to number 1 on the charts. The song was still at number 3 when their next hit, "Dedicated" hit the Top Ten. The Shirelles would hit the pop charts twenty-six times and the R&B charts twenty times. Before long, every songwriter in the business was trying to get them to record a song.

Doris left the group in 1968, shrinking the Shirelles to a trio. In 1969 a rock and roll revival began, which gave them an expanded audience. Although they were still touring and recording, their earlier hits put rock nostalgia on their side. The group continued to perform through the '70s and into the early '80s, with Doris back in the ranks. On June 10, 1982, Mickey Harris died of a heart attack while on-stage in Atlanta. In the early '90s there were three different groups going by the name the Shirelles, each with one original member of the group.

SISTER SLEDGE

The singers of Sister Sledge were the reigning queens of the Philadelphia disco scene in the late '70s. Four sisters, Kathie, Joni, Kim and Debra Sledge grew up with performers for parents and a former opera singer for a grandmother. The group evolved through several names before arriving at Sister Sledge. The girls first hit the charts in 1974, at ages fifteen to twenty. But it wasn't until their rousing "We Are Family" went to number 2 on the pop charts in 1979 that they became a household name. The song became the theme of the Pittsburgh Pirates in 1979, and was later adopted as an unofficial gay anthem. The sisters continued to record and score hits, but motherhood and the demise of the disco era brought an end to the group. Kathy eventually went solo. In 1991 the remaining trio of sisters recorded an album of dance music in Europe.

SPICE GIRLS

A manufactured group of girl singers groomed and trained to create an image and perform for teens sounds a lot like the girls groups of the late '50s and early '60s. In the case of the Spice Girls it was the same story in a new decade. Auditions were held in March of 1993 for an all-girl pop group. The chosen performers were Victoria Addams, Melanie Chisolm, Geri Halliwell, Melanie Brown and Michelle Stevenson. Michelle just didn't fit the group's image and left in May to be replaced by Emma Bunton. The girls were housed together in Maidenhead, England, where they underwent rigorous training. The group was called Touch at this point, but soon changed its name to Sugar 'n' Spice. By October of 1993 the girls were fed up with being told what to sing and what to wear, so they left their manager and took control. With their first single, "Wannabe," the Spice Girls became famous around the world. Their second single, "Say You'll Be There," went to the top of the charts in fifty countries. Using the alter-ego names Sporty, Scary, Baby Sexy, Ginger and Posh, the group adopted a bold, "girl power" stance, even making a movie. Geri Halliwell left in May of 1998, but the group continued as a quartet.

THE SUPREMES

The Supremes, later billed as Diana Ross & The Supremes, was the flashiest and most successful female group of the '60s. They scored an amazing twelve number 1 hit singles. At the height of the American Civil Rights movement, these women were seen as icons of African-American achievement. Unlike most of their female Motown colleagues, the Supremes' image was sophisticated. They appealed to adults and teens, blacks and whites alike. The Supremes were fronted by Diana Ross in their heyday. Ross and singers Mary Wilson and Florence Ballard met while living in Detroit housing projects. They began singing together as the Primettes in 1959, along with Betty McGlown and later Brenda Martin, while still in their teens. They recorded briefly for LuPine in 1960. While Berry Gordy Jr.'s Motown machine groomed all its performers to fit a polished mold (there were actually required classes at Motown in grooming), Gordy paid special attention to the Supremes, particularly to Diana Ross. It wasn't until their tenth release, "Where Did Our Love Go" that the girls hit number 1 in 1964, which was quite a feat in that Beatles-crazed year. They scored two more chart toppers with "Baby Love" and "Come See About Me" before the year was out. In 1965 it was "Stop! In the Name of Love," followed by numerous other classic hits.

The Supremes' cultivation of a wide audience base and a sophisticated image coincided with the changing times of the 1960s. They broke television taboos, appearing on such mainstream programs as "The Ed Sullivan Show," "The Tonight Show" and "The Hollywood Palace," and were even given their own network TV special. Although they had begun as a group, it soon became clear that Diana Ross was the star, and Gordy began making plans for her solo career. Ballard left the group in 1967, replaced by Cindy Birdsong, formerly of Patti LaBelle & The Blue Belles. But the Motown production team that had handled the Supremes had changed, and other things were changing as well. Ross recorded a couple of songs with anonymous backup singers, still using the Supremes' name. When she left to go solo in 1969, she was replaced by Jean Terrell. Although Ross' superstar solo career was enormously successful, the new Supremes beat her on the charts at first. The last incarnation of the original Supremes gave a farewell performance in London in 1977. Several previous members came together in the following years to perform under their famous name. Since the personnel changes began in the 1960s, there has always been some publicly professed resentment by former members. In 1986 the drama of the unofficial quasi-Supremes' story hit Broadway in the form of the musical *Dreamgirls*.

WILSON PHILLIPS

Rock's "Generation Next," Wilson Phillips sported a notable lineage. Members Wendy and Carnie Wilson are daughters of the Beach Boys' Brian Wilson, while Chynna Phillips calls Michelle and John Phillips of The Mamas & The Papas mom and pop. The rich harmonies of the girls' 1990 debut album went to number 2 on the charts, followed by a disappointing *Shadows and Light* album in 1992. Although it hit number 4 and went platinum, not one song from the album became a hit single. The group disbanded the following year.

TLC

Formed in 1991, this trio of singers from Atlanta consists of Tionne "T-boz" Watkins, Lisa "Left Eye" Lopes and Rozanda "Chili" Thomas. The girls were twenty-one and working blue-collar jobs in Atlanta when singer/producer Perri "Pebbles" Reid and R&B man Dallas Austin brought them together. Husky vocals combined with the sounds of rap and R&B, as well as aggressive performances, gave the group their distinctive flavor. The girls soon developed a style, sound and determination that lifted them above their manufactured beginnings. Financial troubles and individual projects put the group into a three-year hiatus, followed by the hit album *Fan Mail* in 1999. This album, even more aggressive than their previous work, sold over half a million copies in its first two weeks on the street.

MY BOYFRIEND'S BACK

Words and Music by ROBERT FELDMAN,
GERALD GOLDSTEIN and RICHARD GOTTEHRER

Moderately

G
C
(Hey, la - di -
You've been spread - in' lies that I was un - true.
gon - na be sor - ry you ev - er were born.
D7
G
la, My boy - friend's back)
So look out now 'cause he's com - in' af - ter you.
'Cause he's kind of big and he's aw - ful strong.
C
D7
G
(Hey, la - di - la, My boy-friend's back)
And he
And he
C
D7
G
C
D7
knows that you've been try - in', and he knows that you've been ly - in',
knows a - bout your cheat - in', now you're gon - na get a beat - in',

C
(Ah -
What made you think he'd be - lieve all yours lies?
G
Am
G
C
oo Ah - oo)
You're a big man now but he'll
G
A
D7
(Ah - oo)
cut you down to size!
Wait and see!
My
G
boy - friend's back, He's gon - na save my rep - u - ta - tion.

C
D7
(Hey, la - di - la, My boy-friend's back)
If
I were you I'd take a per - ma - nent va - ca - tion.
C
D7
G
(Hey, la - di - la, My boy-friend's back)
La - di -
C
D7
G
C
D7
Repeat and Fade
la, My boy-friend's back! La - di - la, My boy-friend's back!

C'EST LA VIE

Words and Music by RAY HEDGES, MARTIN BRANNIGAN,
TRACY ACKERMAN and B*WITCHED

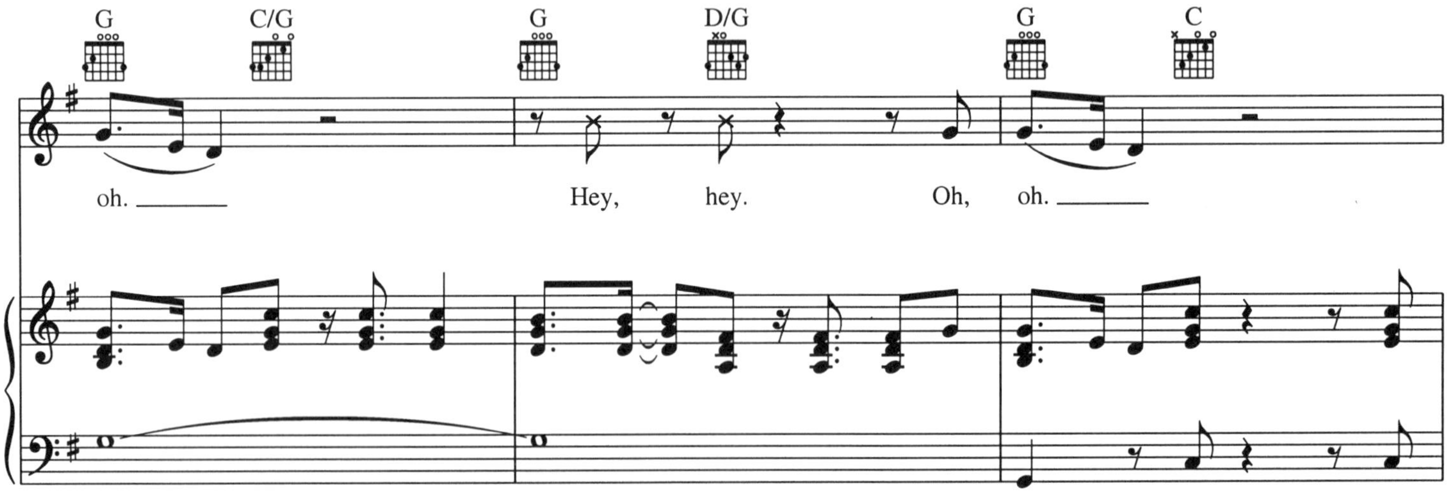

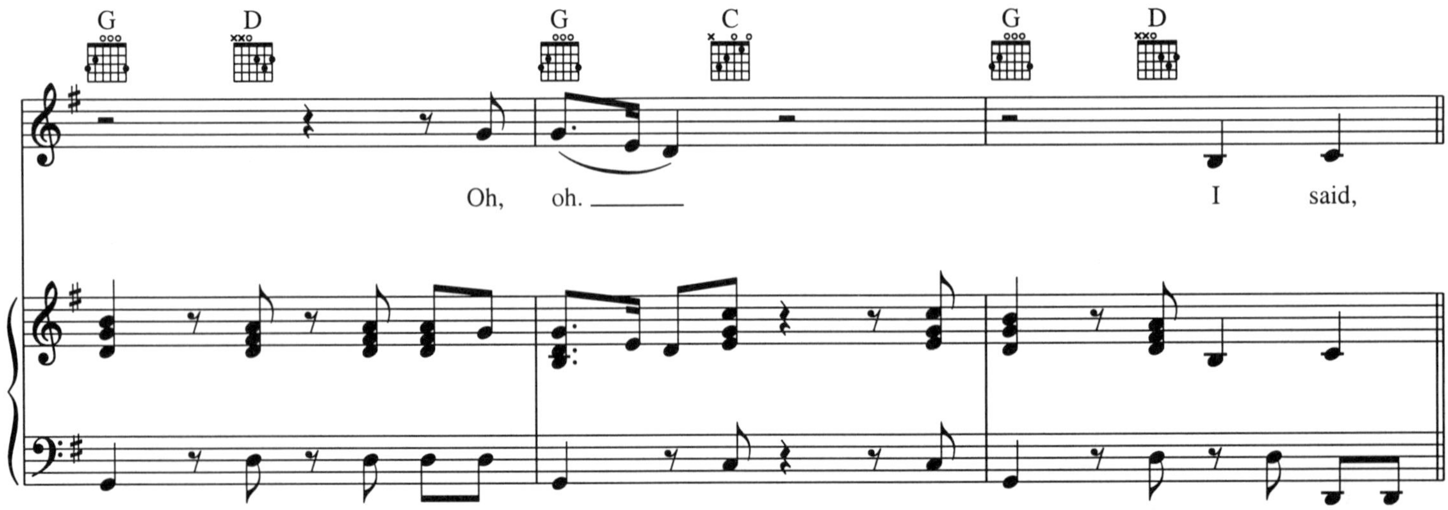

N.C.
hey, boy, sit-tin' in your tree, mom-my al-ways wants you to come for tea.
play with the girls, play with the boys? Do you ev - er get lone - ly play-in' with your toys?
Don't be shy. Straight-en up your tie. Get down from the tree - house, sit - tin' in the sky.
We can talk, we can sing. I'll be the queen and you'll be the king.
I wan-na know just what I do. Is it ver - y big? Is there room for two?
Hey, boy, in your tree, throw down your lad-der. Make-a room for me.
I got a house with a - win-dows and doors. I'll show you mine if you show me yours.

Em7
A7
C/D
Got - ta let _ me in, _ hey, hey, hey. Let the fun _ be - gin, _
G
Em7
A7
hey. _ I'm the wolf _ to - day, _ hey, hey, hey. I'll
Cm7
3 fr
huff, I'll puff. I'll huff, I'll puff. I'll blow you a - way. _
Say you will, _
G
C
G
D
Say you'll do _ what I don't. Say you're true, _
_ say you won't.

G C G D G C
say to me c'est la vie. Say you will, say you won't. Say you'll do
G D G C
what I don't. Say you're true, say to me
1
G D
c'est la vie.
Do you
2
G D
c'est la vie.
N.C.
A D
Instrumental solo
A E A D A E
Hey, hey, na, na, na, ay.

A D A E
Na, na, na, oh. Na, na, na, ay,
A D A E
Hey, hey, hey, hey. Say you will,
Solo ends.
A D A E
say you won't. Say you'll do what I don't. Say you're true,
A D A E
say to me. Wan - na say c'est la vie. Say you will,

A D A E
say you won't. Say you'll do what I don't. Say you're true,
A D A E
c'est la vie.
say to me Na, na, na, ay.
A D A E
C'est la vie.
Na, na, na, oh. Na, na, na, ay.
A D A E A
Hey, hey. C'est la vie.

ETERNAL FLAME

Words and Music by BILLY STEINBERG,
TOM KELLY and SUSANNA HOFFS

Original key: F♯ major. This edition has been transposed up one half-step to be more playable.

1
D
Bm
Am7
dream - in'? Is this burn - ing an e - ter - nal flame?
2
D
Bm7
2 fr
Am7
dream - ing? Or is this burn - ing an e - ter - nal flame?
D
Dm
G/D
D
Say my name, the sun shines through the rain, a whole
F
G
C
G/B
Am7
life so lone - ly, you come and ease the pain.

D
Bm7
2fr
F/C
C
I don't wan - na lose this feel - ing,
1
Dsus
D
Em
B7
Em
A7
oh.
D
Bm7
2fr
Am7
2
D
D.S. al Coda
ah.

CODA
D
Bm7
2 fr
Am7
dream - ing? Or is this burn - ing
G
Em
an e - ter - nal flame?
C
D
G
Em
Oh,
oh.
C
D
G
rit.

WALK LIKE AN EGYPTIAN

Words and Music by
LIAM STERNBERG

2, 4, 7
F5
on your cig - a - rette. For - eign types with the hook - ah pipes _ say,
an E - gyp - ti - an. All the kids in the mar - ket - place _ say,
like E - gyp - ti - ans. All the cops in the do - nut shop _ say,
"Way oh way oh, _ way _ oh
way oh." _
N.C.
To Coda
1
D.C.
Walk like an E - gyp - tian.

2
E♭
3fr
Guitar solo
C

E♭
3 fr
N.C.
Solo ends

Additional Lyrics

3. The blond waitresses take their trays.
   They spin around and they cross the floor.
   They've got the moves, oh way oh.
   You drop your drink, then they bring you more.

4. All the schoolkids so sick of books,
   They like the punk and the metal band.
   Then the buzzer rings, oh way oh,
   They're walking like an Egyptian.

5. Slide your feet up the street, bend your back.
   Shift your arm, then you pull it back.
   Life's hard, you know, oh way oh,
   So strike a pose on a Cadillac.

6. If you want to find all the cops,
   They're hanging out in the donut shop.
   They sing and dance, oh way oh.
   They spin the club, cruise down the block.

7. All the Japanese with their yen,
   The party boys call the Kremlin.
   And the Chinese know, oh way oh,
   They walk the line like Egyptians.

ONE FINE DAY

Words and Music by GERRY GOFFIN
and CAROLE KING

F
Dm11
Dm7
be.
your side.
be - fore.
One fine day
B♭
C7
To Coda
1 F
you're gon - na want me for your girl.
Dm
B♭
Csus
2 F
B♭
F
girl.

Cm7 F/G Cm7 F Cm F6
3 fr
Though I know you're the
Cm7 F/G Cm7 F Cm7 F
kind of boy
B♭ B♭maj7
who on - ly wants to run a -
B♭6 B♭(add9) Dm7 D7sus/A Dm7
6 fr
round. I'll keep

G Dm7 G6 Dm7 D7sus/A Dm7 G F/G G
wait - ing, and some - day dar - ling,
D.S. al Coda
C B♭/C Gm7/C B♭/C C
you'll come to me when you want to set - tle down, oh.
CODA
F Dm11 5 fr Dm7
girl. One fine day,
B♭ C F
oh, oh, one fine

Dm11
5fr
Dm7
B♭
C
day ___ you're gon - na want me for your
F
Dm7
girl.
Shoo - be - do - be - do - be - do - be - do wah, wah,
Lead vocal 1st time only
B♭
Gm7/C
shoo - be - do - be - do - be - do - be - do wah, wah.
F
Dm7
B♭
B♭/C
Repeat and Fade
Instrumental ad lib. and fade

SWEET TALKIN' GUY

Words and Music by DOUG MORRIS, ELLIOT GREENBERG,
BARBARA BAER and ROBERT SCHWARTZ

Fm6/A♭
6fr
C/G
He'll send you flow - ers, then paint the town with an - oth - er girl.
(D.S.) Don't give him love to - day. To - mor - row he's on his way.
G7
He's a sweet talk - in' guy, but he's
my kind of guy!
To Coda
C
Sweet - er than su - gar,
G/B
kiss - es like wine.
B♭dim
Don't let him

F/A
D.S. al Coda
un - der your skin 'cause you'll nev - er win.
CODA
Eb 3fr
Ab 4fr
Db
G
Why do I love him like I do?
C
G
Stay a - way from him.
Gdim
F
D.S. and Fade
No, you'll nev - er win.

MISTER SANDMAN

Lyric and Music by
PAT BALLARD

C7
F7
Give him two lips like ros - es in clo -
Give him the word that I'm not a ro -
Bb6
Gbmaj9
3fr
- ver,
- ver,
Then tell me that my lone - some nights are
F9
Bb
o - ver.
Sand - man,
A7
D7
I'm so a - lone,
Don't have no -

G7
bod - y to call my own.
Cm7
Please turn on your mag - ic
E♭m6/G♭
beam,
B♭/F
C9/E
F7
B♭
Mis - ter Sand - man, bring me a dream.
1
Fdim7
L.H.
F13
Mis - ter
2
F13
B♭6/9
L.H.

CHAINS

Words and Music by GERRY GOFFIN
and CAROLE KING

A
see. free.
Wo, these Wo, these
E9
D9
chains of love got a hold on
chains of love won't let me
A
To Coda
1
E7
2-3
A7
me, yeah.
be, yeah.
D7
I wan - na tell you pret - ty ba - by,
Please be - lieve me when I tell you,

A
A7
D
I think you're fine. I'd like to
your lips are sweet. I'd like to
E
love you, but dar - ling, I'm im -
kiss them, but I can't break a -
1
2
D.S. al Coda
CODA
E7
pris - oned by these
way from all of these
A
Repeat and Fade
Chains. Chains of love.

UPTOWN

Words and Music by BARRY MANN
and CYNTHIA WEIL

C
Am
up - town each eve-ning to my ten - e - ment, _ up - town where folks don't have to
up - town where he can hold his head up high, _ up - town he knows that I'll be
F
pay much rent. _ And when he's there with me, he can see that he's ev - ery - thing. _
stand - in' by. _ And when I take his hand, there's no man who can put him down. _
Am
A♭
4fr
Then he's tall, he don't
The world is sweet, it's at his
Fm7
To Coda
1
C
crawl, he's a king. _
feet when he's up -

2
C
Am
town,
oh.
F
G
D.S. al Coda
CODA
C
Am
town,
oh,
oh.
C
Am
Repeat ad lib. and Fade
Oh,
oh.

HE'S SURE THE BOY I LOVE

Words and Music by BARRY MANN
and CYNTHIA WEIL

Spoken ad lib.

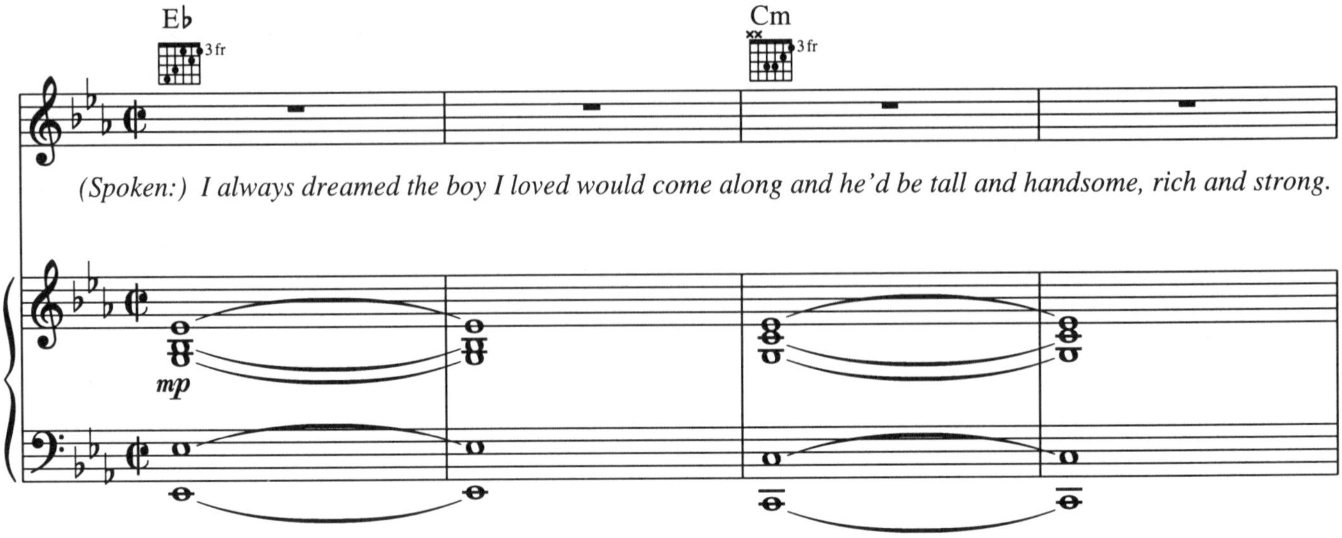

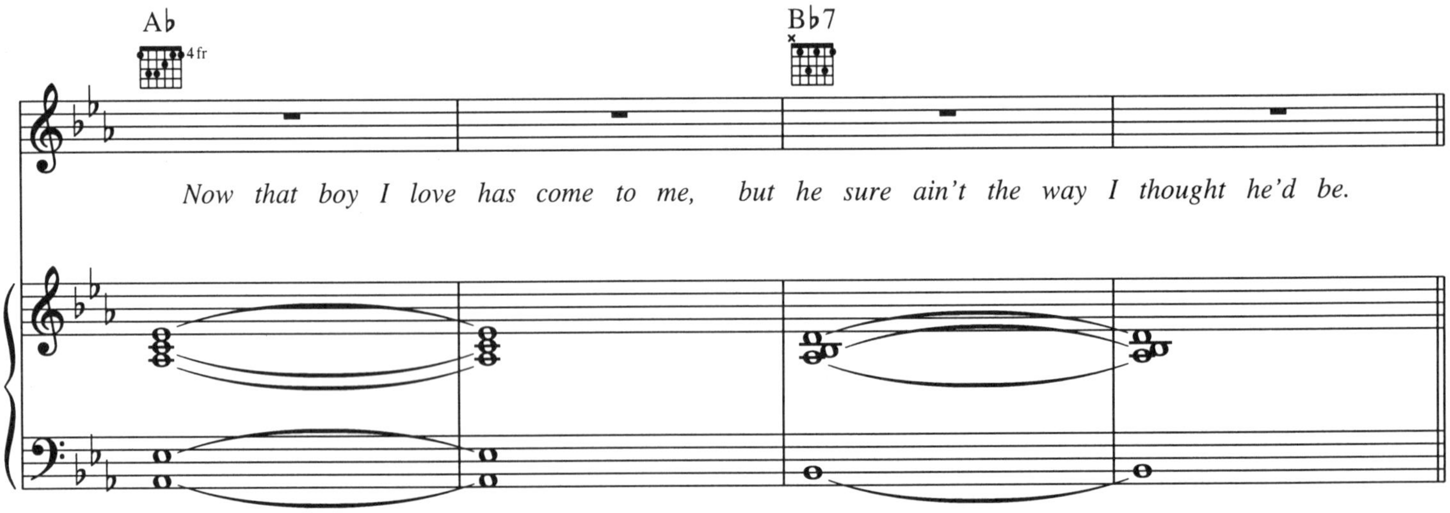

Moderately slow, in rhythm

A♭
4 fr
Cad - il - lac car, he sure ain't the boy I've been
B♭7
dream - in' of, but he's sure the boy I love.
E♭
3 fr
B♭7
E♭
3 fr
Let me tell ya now, he'll nev - er be a big
Cm
3 fr
bus - 'ness man, he al - ways buys on the in -

A♭
stall - ment plan, he sure ain't the boy I've been
B♭7
dream - in' of, but he's sure the boy I love.
E♭
Gm
A♭
'Cause when he holds me tight, ev - 'ry-thing's right,
3
3
Gm
A♭
E♭
cra - zy as it seems. I'm his, what -

B♭7
A♭
B♭7
ev - er he is, and I for - get all of my dreams. Now ev - 'ry bod - y knows that
E♭
Cm
he does - n't hang dia - monds 'round my neck and all he's got's an un - em -
A♭
ploy - ment check. He sure ain't the boy I've been dream - in' of, but
B♭7
1
E♭
B♭7
2
E♭
he's sure the boy I love.

BILLS, BILLS, BILLS

Words and Music by KANDI L. BURRUSS,
KEVIN BRIGGS, BEYONCE KNOWLES,
KELLY ROWLAND and LE TOYA LUCKETT

Em7
F♯
you're get - ting comf' - ta - ble, ain't do - in' those things you did no more. You're
Have - n't paid the first bill, but you're stead - y head - in' to the mall, goin' on
Em7
F♯
slow - ly mak - in' me pay for things your mon - ey should be han - dl - ing.
shop - pin' sprees per - pe - trat - in' to your friends that you be ball - in'.
Bm
F♯
Bm
And now you ask to use my car. Drive it all day and don't fill
And then you use my cell - phone, call - in' who - ev - er that you
F♯
Em7
up the tank. And you have the au - dac - i - ty to
think at home. And then when the bill comes, all of a

F#
Em7
e - ven come and step to me and ask to hold some mon - ey from me un -
sud - den you back act - in' dumb. Don't know where none of those calls come from when your
F#
Bm
til you got your check next week.
ma - ma's num - ber's here more than once.
You tri - fl - in'
F#
Bm
good - for - noth - in' type of broth - er. Sil - ly me, why
F#
Em7
have - n't I found an - oth - er? A ball - er, when times get hard

F♯
Em7
need some-one to help me out, in - stead of a scrub like you
F♯
Bm
who don't know what a man's a - bout. Can you pay my bills? Can you
A♯dim
A
pay my tel - e-phone bills? Do you pay my au - to-mo-bills? If you
E/G♯
N.C.
G
did then may - be we could chill. I don't think you do, so

F♯
N.C.
you and me are through.
Bm
Can you pay my bills? Can you
A♯dim
pay my tel - e-phone bills?
A
Do you pay my au - to-mo-bills? If you
E/G♯
did then may - be we could chill.
N.C.
I don't think you
G
F♯
N.C.
do, so you and me are through.

Bm
A♯dim
You tri - fl - in' good - for - noth - in' type of broth - er.
Bm
A♯dim
Play 4 times
Oh, sil - ly me, why have - n't I found an - oth - er?
Bm
A♯dim
Can you pay my bills? Can you pay my tel - e-phone bills? Do you
Lead vocal ad lib
A
E/G♯
pay my au - to - mo - bills? If you did than may - be we could chill.

N.C.
G
F♯
N.C.
Play 3 times
I don't think you do, so you and me are through.
N.C.
Can you pay my bills? Can you pay my tel - e-phone bills? Do you
pay my au - to-mo-bills? If you did then may - be we could chill.
I don't think you do, so you and me are through.

READY TO RUN

Words and Music by MARTIE SEIDEL
and MARCUS HUMMON

C G C G D
read - y this time. When my mom said I look good in white,
C G
I'm gon - na be read - y this time,
C G Bm C
oh, yeah. Read - y, read - y, read - y, read - y read - y to run.
D Bm C
All I'm read - y to do is have some

D
C/E
F
D/F#
fun.
What's all this talk a - bout
G
Gsus
3fr
D
N.C.
love?
I feel the wind blow through my hair.
D7
C
G
C
G
I'm gon-na be read - y this time.
I buy a
D
D7
tick - et to an - y - where.
Gon - na be

C G C G
read - y this time. You see, it
(read - y this time)
D
feels like I'm start - in' a - gain. And I'm gon - na be
C G C G
read - y this time.
(read - y this time)
Bm C D
Read y,-read - y, read - y, read - y read - y to run.

Bm
C
D
All I'm read - y to do is have some fun.
C/E
F
D/F#
G
N.C.
What's all this talk a - bout love?
I'm read - y to run,
G5
3 fr
I'm read - y to run,
oh.

Bm
C
D
Read-y, read-y, read-y, read-y ready-y to run.
Bm
C
D
All I'm read-y to do is have some fun.
C/E
F
D/F♯
N.C.
G5
3 fr
What's all this talk a-bout love
I'm read-y to run,

I'm read - y to run,
I'm read - y to run,
I'm read - y to run,
C G D G
I'm read - y to run,
oh,
3

C G D G
ready to run, yeah,
C G D G
I'm ready to run.
C G D G C G D
I'm read - y, oh, I'm ready to run,
G C G D G
I'm read - y, ready to run, I'm read - y,

C G D G
oh, I'm read - y to run, I'm read - y.
C G D G
C G D/A G/B C G D
Repeat and Fade
N.C.
Optional Ending
G5
3 fr

WIDE OPEN SPACES

Words and Music by
SUSAN GIBSON

F♯m7
E/G♯
Who's nev - er left home, who's nev - er struck out to find a
A
E
A
dream and a life of their own, a place in the clouds, a foun - da -
A/B
B
E
F♯m7
tion of stone?
Man - y pre - cede and man - y will
She trav - eled this road as a
E
F♯m7
fol - low, a young girl's dreams no long - er
child, wide - eyed and grin - ning, she nev - er
3

E A E
hol - low. It takes the shape of a place out west.
tired. But now she won't be com - ing back with the
A
But what it holds for her she has - n't yet
rest. If these are life's les - sons, she'll take this
A/B B E F#m7
guessed.
test.
She needs wide o - pen spac -
A B E F#m7
- es, room to make her big mis -

A
B
E
F♯m7
- takes. She needs new fac -
es. She knows the high stakes.
1
2
stakes. She know the high stakes.

F♯m7
E
F♯m7
E
F♯m7
A/B
E
A/C♯
E
As her folks drive a-way, her dad yells, "Check the oil."
A/C♯
E
Mom stares out the win-dow and says, "I'm leav-in' my girl."
She said, "It

A E A
didn't seem like that long a - go" when she stood there and let her own
A/B B E F#m7 A B
folks know she need - ed wide o - pen spac - es,
E F#m7 A B
room to make her big mis - takes. She needs
E F#m7 A B
new fac - es. She knows the high

E F#m7 A B E F#m7
stakes. She knows the high stakes, she knows the high stakes. Wide o - pen spac -
A B E F#m7
- es, she knows the high stakes,
A B E F#m7 A B
she knows the high stakes, wide o - pen spac - es.
E F#m7 A A/B E

YOU WERE MINE

Written by MARTIE SEIDEL
and EMILY ERWIN

E/G♯ E F♯m7 D
to hang on. What went wrong can be for-giv - en. With-out
have be - gun to fade. Please tell me she's not real and that you're
F♯m7 D A
you, it ain't worth liv - in' a - lone.
real - ly com - in' home to stay.
Some - times
E D A D
I wake up cry - in' at night. And some - times
E D A
I scream out your name. What right

E
D
A
does she have to take
you a - way
your heart a - way
when for so
Bm7
2 fr
D
1
E
2
E
D
long you were mine
I
G
D/F#
I can give you two good rea - sons to
F
C
show you love's not blind.
He's

A E/G♯ F♯m D A/C♯
two and she's four and you know they a - dore you. So,
Bm7 A/C♯ D E
2 fr
how can I tell them you've changed your mind Some - times
F♯ E B E/G♯
I wake up cry - in' at night and some - times
F♯ E B
I scream out your name. What right

F♯
E
B/D♯
4 fr
B
does she have to take your heart a - way when for so
C♯m7
4 fr
E
F♯
long you were mine?
I re - mem -
C♯m7
4 fr
E
F♯
B
E
- ber when you were mine.
Gm7
Esus2
Emaj7
B

FREE YOUR MIND

Words and Music by THOMAS McELROY
and DENZIL FOSTER

G5 G♯5 A5
3 fr 4 fr 5 fr
I like rap mu - sic, wear hip - hop clothes. That does - n't mean that I'm out
So why dis - pute me and waste my time be - cause you real - ly think the
sell - in' dope, no, no, no. Oh, my! For - give me for
price is high for me? I can't look
hav - ing straight hair. No, it does - n't mean there's an - oth - er
with - out be - ing watched, no. You rang my buy be - fore I
blood in my heirs, yeah, yeah. I might date an - oth - er
rang up my mind. Oh! Oh, now at - ti - tude,

G5 G#5 A5
G5 G#5 A5
race or col - or. It does - n't mean I don't like my
why e - ven both - er? I can't change your mind,
G5 G#5 A5
Dm C
strong black broth - ers.
you can't change my col - or.
Ooh,
G/B Gm/B♭
A5 G5 G#5 A5
G5 G#5 A5
Why, oh why must it be this way?
Dm C G/B Gm/B♭
Ah. Be -

fore you can read me, you've got to learn how to see me. I said:
Am
Free your mind and the rest will fol - low. Be
col - or - blind, don't be so shal - low.
Free your mind and the rest will fol - low. Be

1
col - or - blind, don't be so shal - low.
2,3
be so shal - low. Free your mind and the
rest will fol - low. Be col - or - blind, don't
be so shal - low. Free your mind and the

rest will fol - low. Be col - or - blind, don't
be so shal - low. Free your mind!
To Coda
N.C.
Play 7 times
(Drum break)
A5 G5 G#5 A5
5 fr 3 fr 4 fr 5 fr
G5 G#5 A5
3 fr 4 fr 5 fr
G5 G#5 A5
3 fr 4 fr 5 fr
1
G5 G#5 A5
3 fr 4 fr 5 fr
2
N.C.
D.S. al Coda
(take 2nd ending)
(Drum break)
CODA
N.C.
Free your mind!

MY LOVIN'

Words and Music by THOMAS McELROY
and DENZIL FOSTER

B♭m6
6fr
love.) never ever gonna get it. (Ooh, bop.) I
(Ooh, bop.) Now
(Ooh, bop.)
re - mem - ber how it used to be. You
you prom - ise me the moon and stars.
(Spoken:) Woo! Yes sir. I give to the needy and
nev - er was this nice; you can't fool me. (Ooh, bop.) Now
Save your breath; you won't get ver - y far. (Ooh, bop.) Gave
not the greedy. Mm hmm, that's right. 'Cause you see, baby,
you're talk - in' like you made a change, the
you man - y chanc - es to make change; the
when you're lockin', you're losin', and

Eb9 Cm7 F7sus
more you talk, the more things sound the same. (1.) What makes you think
on - ly thing you changed was love to hate. (2., D.S.) It does - n't mat -
I'm out the door!
Bbm Eb9 Cm7 F7sus
you can just walk back in - to her life with - out a
- ter what you do or what you say; she does - n't
Bbm Eb9 Cm7 F7sus
good fight? Oh. I just sit back
love you, no way. May - be next
Bbm Eb9 Cm7 F7sus
To Coda
and watch you make a fool of your-self, 'cause you're just wast-ing your time. Oh.
time you'll give your wom - an a lit-tle re - spect so you won't be hear-ing her say, "No way."

B♭m6
6fr
No, you're nev-er gon-na get it, (Not _ this time.) _ nev-er ev-er gon-na get it. (My
lov - in'.) No, you're nev-er gon-na get it, nev - er ev-er gon - na get it.
(Had your chance _ to make _ a change.) _
No, you're nev-er gon-na get it, (Not _ this time.) _ nev-er ev-er gon-na get it. (My
lov - in'.) No, you're nev-er gon-na get it, nev-er ev-er gon-na get it.
(Had _ your chance _ to make _ a change.) _

Bbm6
6fr
No, you're nev-er gon-na get it, (Not this time.) nev-er ev-er gon-na get it. (My
lov - in'.) No, you're nev-er gon-na get it,
1
nev - er ev-er gon - na get it.
(Had your chance to make a change.)
2
D.S. al Coda
nev - er ev-er gon - na get it.
(Had your chance to make a change.)
CODA
Bbm
N.C.
(Spoken:) And now it's time for a break down.
Shuffle feel
Bbm
F+/C
Db
Bb/D
Eb
3fr
Gdim/Db
Ab/C
3fr
Abm/Cb
Bbm
Nev-er gon-na get it, nev-er gon-na get it. Nev - er gon-na get it, nev-er gon-na get it. Nev -

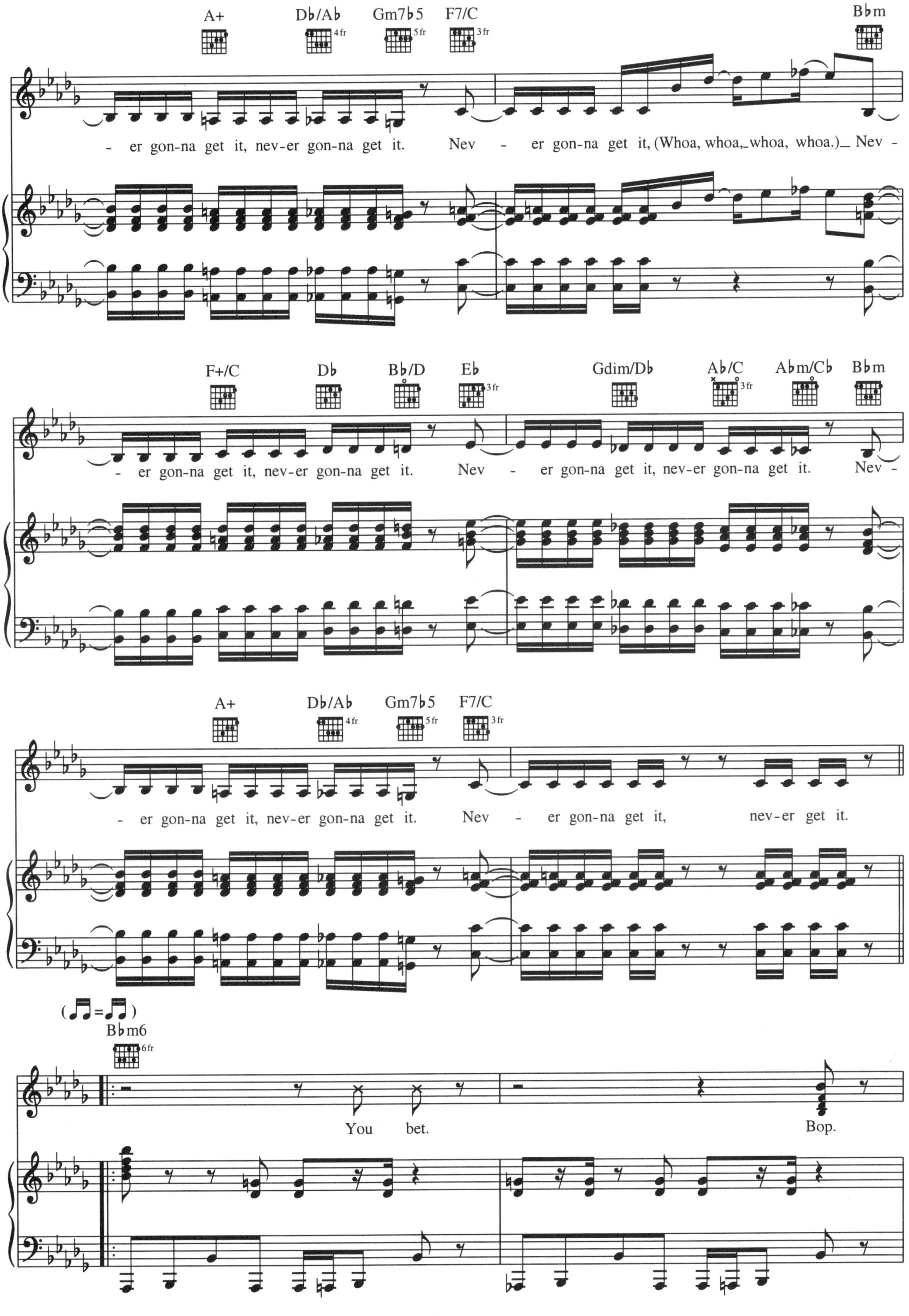
A+ Db/Ab Gm7b5 F7/C Bbm
- er gon-na get it, nev-er gon-na get it. Nev - er gon-na get it, (Whoa, whoa,_whoa, whoa.)_ Nev -
F+/C Db Bb/D Eb Gdim/Db Ab/C Abm/Cb Bbm
- er gon-na get it, nev-er gon-na get it. Nev - er gon-na get it, nev-er gon-na get it. Nev -
A+ Db/Ab Gm7b5 F7/C
- er gon-na get it, nev-er gon-na get it. Nev - er gon-na get it, nev-er get it.
Bbm6
You bet. Bop.

You bet.
Bop.
B♭m6
6fr
No, you're nev-er gon-na get it, (Sweet lov - in'.) nev-er ev-er gon-na get it. (Sweet
lov - in'.) No, you're nev-er gon-na get it, (My lov - in'.) nev-er ev-er gon-na get it. (My
Repeat ad lib. and Fade
Optional Ending
B♭m
lov - in'.) No, you're nev-er gon-na get it, (Sweet lov - in'.) nev-er ev-er gon-na get it. (My lov - in'.)

WE GOT THE BEAT

Words and Music by
CHARLOTTE CAFFEY

fall in line just watch - ing all their feet. They don't know where
They can't wait to hang out and be cool. Hang a - round 'til quar -
Do the po - ny; puts us in a trance. Do the watusi, just
they want to go, but they walk - ing in time. They
ter af - ter twelve. That's when they fall in line They got the beat,
give us a chance. That's when we fall in line. 'Cause we
D
G
F
To Coda
they got the beat, they kids we got the beat,

1
C
2
C
A(no3rd)
yeah, they got the beat.
yeah, kids got the beat.
B

D.S. al Coda
CODA
C
yeah, we got it!
no chord
play 3 times
A(no3rd)
(We got the beat.) Ev - 'ry - bod - y
get off your feet. (We got the beat.) We know you can
dance to the beat. (We got the beat.) Jump back,

E
get down.
(We got the beat.)
'Round and 'round and 'round.
A(no3rd)
(We got the beat.)
We got the beat. (We got the beat.)
We got the beat.
(We got the beat.)
(We got the beat.) We got the beat.
(We got the beat.)
(We got the beat.) We got the beat!

GALILEO

Words and Music by
EMILY SALIERS

F6/9 G7 G6 Am Em(add4)/B
B♭6/9 C7 C6 Dm Am(add4)/E
- ly fears _ ex - plode, _ I try to trace them to my youth. _
_ in your _ life - time. _ Now, I have to pay. _
F6/9 Gsus C Gsus
B♭6/9 Csus F Csus
3 fr
And then you had _ to bring _ up re -
_ (To V.3) And then I think _ a - bout _ my fear _
But then a - gain it feels kike some _ sort of in - spi - ra -
F6/9 Gsus C Gsus
B♭6/9 Csus F Csus
- in - car - na - tion o - ver a cou - ple of _ beers _ the oth - er night. _
_ of mo - tion _ for which I nev - er could ex - plain. _
- tion to let the next life off the hook _
F6/9 Gsus C Gsus
B♭6/9 Csus F Csus
_ And now, I'm serv - ing time for mis -
_ Some oth - er fool a - cross _ the o -
_ or she'll say, "Look what I had to o - ver - come _

F6/9 Gsus Am Em(add4)/B F6/9 Gsus
B♭6/9 Csus Dm Am(add4)/E B♭6/9 Csus
3 fr
takes made _ by an - oth - er in an - oth - er life - time.
- cean years a - go _ must have crashed his lit - tle air - plane. How _
_ in my last _ life. I think I'll write _ a book."_
C Gsus F6/9 Gsus
F Csus B♭6/9 Csus
long till my soul gets _ it right? _ Can an - y hu - man being _
C Gsus F6/9 Gsus Am Em(add4)/B
F Csus B♭6/9 Csus Dm Am(add4)/E
_ ev - er reach _ that kind _ of light? _ I call on _ the rest - ing _ soul _ of
that kind _ of light? _ I call on _
the high - est light _ ex - cept for _
D13 F6/9 Gsus C Gsus
G13 B♭6/9 Csus F Csus
2 fr
To Coda
1
Gal - i - le - o, king of night _ vi - sion, king of in - sight. _

F6/9 Gsus
B♭6/9 Csus
2 C Am F/A
F Dm B♭/D
— sight. — I'm not mak-ing a joke. —
F♯dim/A F/A
Bdim/D B♭/D
— You know me, I take ev - e-ry-thing — so ser - i-ous-ly. If we
Am F/A Gsus F6/9
Dm B♭/D Csus B♭6/9
wait for the time — till all souls — get it right, then at least I know there'll be no nu-cle-
Gsus C Gsus F6/9 Gsus
Csus F Csus B♭6/9 Csus
ar an-ni-hi-la-tion in my life - time. I'm still — not right. —

G
F
Gsus
Csus
3 fr
F6/9
B♭6/9
Gsus
Csus
3 fr
C
F
Gsus
Csus
3 fr
F6/9
B♭6/9
Gsus
Csus
3 fr
C
F
Gsus
Csus
3 fr
F6/9
B♭6/9
Gsus
Csus
3 fr
Am
Dm
Em(add4)/B
Am(add4)/E
D13
G13
2 fr
F6/9
B♭6/9
Gsus
Csus
3 fr
C
F
Gsus
Csus
3 fr
F6/9
B♭6/9
Gsus
Csus
3 fr
C
F
Gsus
Csus
3 fr

F6/9
B♭6/9
Gsus
Csus
3 fr
D.S. al Coda
CODA
F6/9
B♭6/9
Gsus
Csus
3 fr
vi - sion, king of in -
C
F
Gsus
Csus
F6/9
B♭6/9
Gsus
Csus
C
F
Gsus
Csus
- sight?
How long?
F6/9
B♭6/9
Gsus
Csus
C
F
Gsus
Csus
F6/9
B♭6/9
Gsus
Csus
How long?
How
C
F
Gsus
Csus
F6/9
B♭6/9
Gsus
Csus
C
F
long?

SHAME ON YOU

Intro
Moderately fast Rock

Words and Music by
AMY RAY

Cadd9
D5
Dsus4
E
beau - ti - ful job we done." I say, "let's
of the win - ter - time. But when the
keep fuck - in' up." I said, "Come on
ask me to step out. They say, "We be look -
G
A
Cadd9
D5
put on some tunes, sing a - long and do lit - tle all day.
sum-mer comes ev - 'ry - thing's in bloom and you would - n't know it's there.
down to chi - ca - no cit - y park and wash your blues a - way."
ing for il - le - gal im - mi - grants, can we check your car?"
G
E
A
Go down to the riv - er - side, take off our shoes and
And the white folks like to pre - tend it's not, but their
The beau - ti - ful la - dies walk right by. You know I
I say, "you know, it's fun - ny. I think we were on the same boat back in
D5
D7
E
Chorus
G
A
wash these sins a - way." The riv - er said
mu - sic's in the air. You can hear them sing - ing,
nev - er know what to say to them. And they'll be sing - ing,
six - teen nine - ty - four." And I said,

Cadd9
D5
Dadd4
E
la, la, la, said, shame on you.
The riv - er said,
You can feel them danc -
They'll be danc - ing.
They'll be danc - ing.
G
A
- ing.
Cadd9
D5
To Coda
la, la, la, said, shame on you.
1,2
Dadd4
E
I go down
My friend Tan - ner,
3
Dadd4
E
shame on you.
Interlude
G
A
D7
E7

Guitar Solo
A
Instrumental solo
D5
1-3
E
4
E
D.S. al Coda
Solo ends
Let's go road -
CODA
Dadd4
E
G
A
shame on you.
La, la, la, la
Cadd9
D5
Dadd4
E
Repeat and Fade
shame on you,
shame on you.

A GIRL'S NIGHT OUT

Words and Music by BRENT MAHER
and JEFF HAWTHORNE BULLOCK

Lively Country beat

G Gsus G Gm G Gsus
G Gm G Gsus G Gm
I did my time work - ing all week. To -
You can give me a lit - tle rock and roll, or
G Gsus G Gm C
night's all mine. To - mor - row I'll sleep. I wan - na hear a band
ev - en a waltz with the lights down low. I'll still be danc -
F G Gsus G Gm
with a coun - try sound.
- ing when they close the doors.

G
Gsus
G
A7
I've been
cooped up all week long
B7
I've been work - ing my
C
fin - gers to the bone.
D7
G
Well, it's a girl's night out.

A7
D7
Hon - ey there ain't no doubt. I'm gon - na dance ev - 'ry dance till
G
the boys go home Well, it's
A7
my night to rock. No watch - ing that old clock.
D7
Oh, ain't no doubt. Law - dy, it's a girl's night

G Gsus G Gm G Gsus
out.
G Gm
G
out. Well it's a
girl's night out.
A
Hon - ey there ain't no doubt.
D7
I'm gon - na dance ev - 'ry dance till the boys go home.

G
Well, it's my night to rock.
A
No watch - ing that old clock. Oh,
D7
ain't no doubt. Law - dy it's a girl's night
G
Gsus
out.
G
Gm
G
Gsus
G
Gm
D.S. and Fade

ROCKIN' WITH THE RHYTHM OF THE RAIN

Words and Music by BRENT MAHER
and DON SCHLITZ

Slide on o - ver ba - by, hold me clo - ser; mov - in' to and fro, just sway -
F7
G
in' like a slow freight train rock - in' with the rhy - thm of the rain
C
So let the breeze
Rock - in' with the rhy - thm of the
f
keep blow - in'.
B♭
F
rain that's a - fall - in', night birds a - sing - in' the crick - ets a - call - in',

G
C
Oh my heart will nev - er be the same.
Keep the sweet feel - in' flow - in'.
Whis - per in my ear ba - by, ooh, feels so fine.
Bb
F
Nights like this come once in a life - time. Me and my ba - by rock -
To Coda
G
C
Bb
F
in' with the rhy - thm of the rain.
mf

B♭
G
C
B♭
F
B♭
G
C
Am7
Oh
C
ba - by, hold me tight.

Am7
D
Say you love me, that's all I want to hear
F G
D.S. al Coda
to - night.
CODA
F
G
Me and my ba - by rock - in' with the rhy - thm of the
C
rain.
p
B♭ F B♭ G C
f
3

LADY MARMALADE

Words and Music by BOB CREWE
and KENNY NOLAN

C
Cm7
3 fr
She said, "Hel-lo, hey Joe, you wan-na
Dm7
Gm7
C
give it a go?" Mm hmm. Get - cha get - cha ya ya da
Gm7
C
da. Get-cha get-cha ya ya here.
Gm7
C
Mo - cha choc - o - la - ta ya ya.

Cm7
G5
cues 1st time only
To Coda
Cre - ole La - dy Mar - ma - lade.
Gm7
C
Vou - lez vous cou - cher a - vec moi ce soir?
Vou - lez vous cou - cher a - vec moi?
1
Stayed in her bou - doir while she fresh - ened up;
(Hey sis - ter, go sis - ter, soul sis - ter, go sis - ter.
that boy drank all that mag - no - lia wine. On her
Hey sis - ter, go sis - ter, soul sis - ter, go sis - ter.)

2
Cm7
3 fr
Dm7
black sat - in sheets, I swear he start-ed to freak.
G5
3 fr
F
Gm/D
F/C
Gm/B♭
E♭maj7
3 fr
G
E♭maj7
3 fr
D
Hey, hey, hey

Gm7
C
hey - ey - ey. Seein' her skin, feel - ing silk - y smooth,
Gm7
C
Cm7
3 fr
col - or of ca - fé au lait, made the sav - age beast in - side roar
liv - ing his gray flan - nel life. But when he turns off to sleep, old
Dm7
D
un - til it cried, "More, more, more!"
mem - 'ries keep... more, more, more!
1
Gm7
C
Now he's at home do - ing nine - to - five,

2
D.S. al Coda
CODA
Gm7
C
Vou - lez vous cou - cher a - vec moi
1
Gm7
C
ce soir?
Vou - lez vous cou - cher a - vec moi?
2
Cm7
3fr
G5
3fr
Gm7
Cre - ole La - dy Mar - ma - lade.
Gm7
C
Vou - lez vous cou - cher a - vec moi
ce soir?

Gm7
C
Play 4 times
Gm7
C
Vou - lez vous cou - cher a - vec moi?
Get - cha get - cha ya ya da
da.
Gm7
C
Get - cha get - cha ya ya here.
Gm7
C
Mo - cha choc - o - la - ta ya ya.
Gm7
C
Repeat and Fade
Optional Ending
G5
3fr
Get - cha get - cha ya ya here.

DANCING IN THE STREET

Words and Music by MARVIN GAYE,
IVY HUNTER and WILLIAM STEVENSON

ca - go, down in New Or - leans,
Bal - ti - more and D. C., now.
in New York City - y.
Can't for - get the Mo - tor City - y.
All we need is mu -
A
- sic, sweet mu - sic. There'll be mu - sic ev - 'ry - where.
E7
There'll be swing-ing and sway - ing and re - cords play - ing,

G♯7
4fr
danc - ing in the street oh.
It does - n't mat - ter what
C♯m
4fr
you wear, just as long as you are there,
F♯m
so come on, ev - 'ry guy grab a girl.
B7sus
4fr
B7
Ev - 'ry - where a - round the world they'll be

E7
(Danc - ing in the street.)
danc - ing, they're danc - ing in the street.
1
2
(Danc-ing in the street.)
This is an way down in L. A.,
ev - 'ry day they're danc - ing in the street.
get in time, we're danc - ing in the street.
me and you, we're danc - ing in the street.
Repeat and Fade
(Danc - ing in the street.) Let's form a big, strong line,
(Danc - ing in the street.) A - cross the o - cean blue,
(Danc - ing in the street.)

NOWHERE TO RUN

Words and Music by LAMONT DOZIER,
BRIAN HOLLAND and EDWARD HOLLAND

Ebm/Ab
Db/Ab
Ab
Ebm/Ab
Db/Ab
11 fr
4 fr
running from, it's the heart-break I know will come.
Ab
Ebm/Ab
Db/Ab
Ab
'Cause I know you're no good for me, but you've be-come a
Ebm/Ab
Db/Ab
Ab
part of me. Ev'-ry-where I go, your
face I see. Ev'-ry step I take, you take with me.

Ab
Ebm/Ab
Db/Ab
4 fr
11 fr
No-where to run to, ba - by, No-where to hide.
No-where to run, no-where to hide from you, ba - by.
Got no-where to run to, ba - by, no-where to hide.
Got no-where to run to, ba - by, no-where to hide.
Bb7
(1.,3.) I know you're no good for me,
(2.) I know you're no good for me,
Eb7
To Coda
1
but free of you I'll nev - er be, no. Each night
but you've be - come a part of me.

Ebm/Ab Db/Ab Ab Ebm/Ab Db/Ab
11 fr 4 fr 4 fr 11 fr 4 fr
as I sleep, _ in - to my heart you creep. _
Ab Ebm/Ab Db/Ab Ab
4 fr 11 fr 4 fr 4 fr
I wake up feel - in' sor - ry I met _ you, hop - ing soon _ that
Ebm/Ab Db/Ab Ab
11 fr 4 fr 4 fr
I'll for - get you. When I look in the mir - ror to comb my hair, _
I see your face just a - smil - ing there.

2
Ab
Ebm/Ab
Db/Ab
Ab
Ebm/Ab
Db/Ab
How can I fight a lov - er that should-n't be when it's
Ab
Ebm/Ab
Db/Ab
Ab
so deep, so deep, deep in - side of me?
Ebm/Ab
Db/Ab
Ab
My love reach - es so high I can't get o - ver it.
Ab
It's so wide I can't get a - round it, no. No - where to run,

Eb m/Ab Db/Ab Ab Eb m/Ab Db/Ab
11 fr 4 fr 4 fr 11 fr 4 fr
no-where to hide from you, ba - by.
Ab Eb m/Ab Db/Ab Ab
4 fr 11 fr 4 fr 4 fr
Just can't get a - way from you, ba - by, no mat - ter how I try.
D.S. al Coda
Eb m/Ab Db/Ab
11 fr 4 fr
CODA
Ab Eb m/Ab Db/Ab
4 fr 11 fr 4 fr
No-where to run to, ba - by,
Repeat and Fade
Ab Eb m/Ab Db/Ab Ab Eb m/Ab Db/Ab
4 fr 11 fr 4 fr 4 fr 11 fr 4 fr
no-where to hide. Got no-where to run to, ba - by,

HEATWAVE
(Love Is Like a Heatwave)

Words and Music by EDWARD HOLLAND, LAMONT DOZIER and BRIAN HOLLAND

Gm7
Cm7
and ___ I'm filled with ___ de - sire. ___
yeah, well, ___ I feel that burn - in' flame. ___ Has
stand it, I ain't nev - er felt like this be - fore. Now
yeah, ho, yeah.
Fm7
Gm7
Ab6
Could it be a dev - il in me ___ or is this the way ___ love's sup -
high blood pres - sure got a hold on me ___ or is this the way ___ love's sup -
that fun - ny feel - in' has me a - mazed; ___ I don't know what to ___ do, my
Don't pass up this chance; ___ this time ___ it's a
Bb7
Eb
Ab
Eb
Ab
Eb
Ab
Eb
Ab
posed to be? ___
posed to be? ___
head's in a haze. ___
true ro - mance. ___
It's like a heat - wave burn - in' in my

Eb Ab Eb Ab Eb Ab Eb Ab Eb Ab Eb Ab
heart. I can't keep from cry - in',
Eb Ab Eb Ab Eb Ab Eb Ab
it's tear - in' me a - part.
1-3
Eb
N.C.
When - ev - er he
Some - times I
Yeah, yeah, yeah,
4
Eb
N.C.
Fm7
Gm7
Ab6
Bb7
Eb

PLAYBOY

Words and Music by ROBERT BATEMAN, BRIAN HOLLAND,
WILLIAM STEVENSON and GLADYS HORTON

F
C
F
N.C.
play - boy.) Play - boy, get a - way from my door.
play - boy, find your - self an - oth - er toy,
C
G
F
I heard a - bout the lov - ers you had be - fore. (You took their love for a
'cause this is one heart you won't de - stroy. ('Cause I can't stand for
game of joy,) oh yeah, (and tossed their hearts a - round as though it was a toy, play -
what you're put - tin' down,) oh yeah, (fool - in' a - round with ev - 'ry girl in town, play -
G
F#
1
G
N.C.
2
G
boy.) Well,
boy.) Well,

Am
You ain't say-ing noth-ing in my book, 'cause this is one fish you'll
nev-er, ev-er hook.
F
You left the oth-ers stand-ing with their hearts in pain, and
G
now you're com-ing 'round tryin' to
N.C.
do me the same.
C
So, play-boy, I've
F
seen your kind,
C
win-ning ev-'ry girl
G
with that same old line.

F
(So, play - boy, stay a - way from my door.) Oh yeah. (I know a - bout the lov - ers
G F♯ G N.C.
you had be - fore, play - boy.) Oh, you know { you've got to / you bet - ter }
1
C F
(watch out, here comes that play - boy.)
Yes, you know you've got to
C F C
(watch out, here comes that play - boy.) (watch out, here comes that
Oh, you've got to

F
G
play - boy.) You bet - ter (watch out.) You bet - ter (watch out.)
2
C
F
C
(watch out, here comes that play - boy.) Watch out, here comes that
F
C
F
play - boy.) Watch - a de play - boy, he's bring - ing me false _ joy.
C
F
Repeat and Fade
Optional Ending
C
(Watch out, here comes that play - boy.)
Lead vocal ad lib.

PLEASE MR. POSTMAN

Words and Music by ROBERT BATEMAN,
GEORGIA DOBBINS, WILLIAM GARRETT,
FREDDIE GORMAN and BRIAN HOLLAND

A
N.C.
might-y long time)
man.
Whoa,
yeah.
(since I heard from this boy-friend of mine.)
D
Bm
There must be some word to-day
from my boy-friend so
G
far a-way.
Please, Mis-ter Post-man, look and see;
A
N.C.
D
is there a let-ter, a let-ter for me?
I've been stand-ing here

Bm
waiting, Mister Postman, so, so patiently
G
A
for just a card or just a letter saying he's returning
N.C.
D
(Please, Mister Postman, look and see;)
home to me. Please, Mister Postman. Oh, yeah.
Bm
G
(is there a letter in your bag for me?) ('Cause it's been a
Please, please, Mister Post -

A
N.C.
might-y long time) (since I heard from this boy-friend of mine.)
man. Whoa, yeah.
D
Bm
So man-y days you've passed me by; you saw the tears stand-ing
G
in my eyes. You would-n't stop to make me feel bet - ter
A
N.C.
D
by leav-ing me a card or a let - ter. Please, Mis-ter Post - man,

Bm
look and see; is there a let - ter, oh, yeah, in your bag for me? You know, it's
G
A
been so long, yeah, since I heard from this boy - friend
N.C.
D
(Wait.) (Wait a min-ute, Mis-ter Post - man.)
of mine. You'd bet - ter wait a min-ute, wait a min-ute. Oh, you'd bet-ter
Bm
G
(Wait.) (Wait a min - ute, Mis - ter Post - man.) (Wait.) (Wait a
wait a min-ute. Please, please, Mis - ter Post - man,

A
min - ute, Mis - ter Post - man.)
please check and __ see __ just one more time for me. __ You'd bet - ter
D
Bm
(Wait.) (Wait a min - ute, Mis - ter Post - man) (Wait. Wait a
wait. Wait a min - ute. Wait __ a min - ute, wait a min - ute, wait a min - ute.
G
min - ute, Mis - ter Post - man.) (Wait.) (Wait a min - ute, Mis - ter Post - man.)
Please, __ Mis - ter Post - man. De -
Repeat ad lib. and Fade
Optional Ending
A
N.C.
D
liv - er de let - ter, the soon - er de bet - ter.

SUGARTIME

Words and Music by CHARLES PHILLIPS
and ODIS ECHOLS

F7
B♭
F
hon - ey in the eve - nin', hon - ey at sup - per time, you'll
C9
C7
F
B♭
F
be my lit - tle hon - ey and love me all the time.
C7
F
C7
F
Put your arms a - round me and swear by the stars a - bove,
C7
F
G7
C7
you'll be mine for - ev - er in a heav - en of love.

F F7 B♭
Sug - ar in the morn - in', sug - ar in the eve - nin', sug - ar at sup - per
F C9 C7
time, be my lit - tle sug - ar and
F B♭ 1 F To Interlude 2 F Fine
love me all the time. Now sug - ar
Interlude
C7 F
time is an - y - time,

C7
that you're near or just ap-
F
C7
pear. So don't you roam,
F
just be my hon-ey-comb. We'll
G7
C7
D.S. al Fine
live in a heav-en of love.

HE'S SO SHY

Words and Music by CYNTHIA WEIL
and TOM SNOW

B♭
Fm
B♭
Some-thing in - side whis-pered to me, "You bet - ter move
And I'm so glad I took the time that I had to
G7
Cm
3 fr
Fm7
in care - ful - ly." And then he smiled and turned a - way;
take to make him mine. He still can do things to my heart
Cm
3 fr
Fm7
B♭
that told me all he could not say. That's when I knew
just like he did right from the start each time I see
Fm
B♭
G7
he want-ed me too, but I'd have to do some break - in' through.
that qual - i - ty that nev - er stops at - tract - ing me.

Cm
Fm7
Ab
He's so shy,
He's so shy, (Yeah, he's so good-looking.)
(D.S.) (Oh, I love my baby.)
Bb
Fm7
Ab
Bb
Eb/Bb
he's so shy, that sweet lit -
he's so shy, (He's really got me goin'.) that sweet lit -
he's so shy, (Oh, he's drivin' me crazy.) that sweet lit -
Ab/C
Eb/Ab
Bb
Cm7
Fm7
- tle boy who caught my eye. He's so shy,
- tle boy who caught my eye. He's so shy,
- tle boy who caught my eye. He's so shy,
Ab
Bb
Fm7
Ab
he's so shy,
(I'm so glad I got to know him,) he's so shy, ('cause he's one in a million)
(I took a long time to know him,) he's so shy, (and I'm so glad I got to show him)

B♭
E♭/B♭
A♭/C
E♭/A♭
B♭
To Coda
and he's much too good to let get by.
and I'll love him till the day I die.
that I'll love him till the day I die.
Whoa, yes he is!
Oh, yes I will!
1
Cm
2
Fm
A♭
B♭
Now hold-ing him
Fm
A♭
B♭
Fm
A♭

D.S. al Coda
Bb
Eb/Ab Bb/Eb
Eb/Ab Bb/Eb
F/G
Cm7
Fm7
3 fr
Ooh, he's so shy,
CODA
Bb
Fm7
Ab
4 fr
Bb
Fm7
Yeah, he's so shy. (Oo - ee, oo - ee, ba - by.)
He's so shy.
Repeat and Fade
Ab
Bb
Fm7
(Oo - ee, oo - ee, ba - by.)
He's so shy.
Optional Ending
Ab
Bb
Eb

I'M SO EXCITED

Words and Music by TREVOR LAWRENCE, JUNE POINTER,
RUTH POINTER and ANITA POINTER

B♭/E♭
E♭
3
E♭/B♭
to - night ___ we'll put ___ all oth - er things _ a - side. _
B♭
Gm7
___ Get in ____ this time ___ and
B♭/C
E♭/C
show me some ___ af - fec - tion, we're
B♭/E♭
E♭
3
E♭/B♭
B♭
go - in' for ___ those pleas - ures in the night. ___
(Instrumental ends)

no chord
Am7
I want to love you, feel you,
Gm7
Dm
Am7
wrap my-self a-round you. I want to squeeze you,
Gm7
please you, I just can't get e-nough. And if you
Cm7
B♭/D
Cm7/F
no chord
move real slow, I'll let it go. I'm so ex-cit-

Gm
3
E♭
3
- ed, and I just can't hide it,
F
I'm a - bout to lose con - trol and I think I like
Gm
3
it! I'm so ex - cit - ed,
E♭
3
and I just can't hide it, and

F
Gm
I know, I know, I know, I know, I know I want you.
We should-n't e - ven think a - bout to - mor-
B♭/C
E♭/C
B♭/E♭
E♭
- row, sweet mem - o - ries will
E♭/B♭
B♭
B♭/A
last a long, long time. We'll

Gm7
B♭/C
E♭/C
have a good ___ time, ___ ba - by, don't ___ you wor - ry,
B♭/E♭
E♭
3
and if we're still play - in' a - round, ___ boy, that's just
E♭/B♭
B♭
no chord
Gm
3
fine. Let's get ex - cit - ed,
E♭
3
we just ___ can't hide ___ it,

E♭
F
Gm
I'm a - bout to lose con - trol ___ and I think I like ___ it!
I'm so ex - cit - ed and I just ___ can't hide _
E♭
E♭
___ it, and I know, I know, I know, _
F
Gm
D.S. and Fade
___ I know, I know I want you, I want you!

JUMP
(For My Love)

Words and Music by MARTI SHARRON,
GARY SKARDINA and STEPHEN MITCHELL

F/G C/G G F/G
I know you like what you see.
G F/G C/D G
Hold me; I'll give you all that you need.
told me I'm the on - ly wom-an for you.
F/G C/D G F/G
Wrap your love a - round me. You're so ex - cit - ed; I can
No - bod - y does you like I do, Then make the move be - fore you
G F/G Dm7 F/C
feel you get - tin' hot - ter, Oh, ba - by! I'll take you down,
turn to go much far - ther, Oh, ba - by! You are the one,

G/C
C/E
F
I'll take you down where no one's ev - er gone be - fore,
you are the one and heav - en waits here at my door,
Dm7
G/B
E/B
And if you want more, if you want more, more, more:
E
A
D/A
E/A
A
Then jump for my love! Jump in
D/A
E/A
A
D/A
E/A
and feel my touch! Jump, if you wan - na taste my

A D/A E/A A
kiss - es in the night! Then jump for my love! Jump!
D/A E/A A D/A E/A
I know my heart can make you hap - py. Jump in! You know these arms can
A D/A E/A A
fill you up. Jump! If you wan - na taste my kiss - es in the night then
D/A E/A A
jump for my love!
1 G

2
A E
You
A E/A C G/C C G/C
When you are next to me, Oh, I
3
G/F C/F G/F C/F E7sus E7
come a - live. Your love burns in -
A E/A A E/A C G/C
side.

C G/C G/F C/F G/F C/F
Oh, it feels so right.
E7sus A D/A E/A
Come to me if you want me to - night.
A D/A E/A A
Jump! Jump in!
D/A E/A A D/A E/B
if you want to taste my kiss - es in the night. Then jump, jump, jump!

A
F
B♭/F
C/F
F
Ooh, yeah you know my heart can make you hap - py. Jump!
B♭/F
C/F
F
B♭/F
You know these arms can fill you up. Jump in! You wan- na taste my
C/F
F
B♭/F
C/F
F
kiss - es in the night! Then jump, jump for my love! Jump!
F
B♭/F
C/F
F
B♭/F
C/F
F
Repeat and Fade

REMEMBER
(Walking in the Sand)

Words and Music by
GEORGE MORTON

G
Cm
B♭
me.
It said that we were through.
A♭
Gm
Fm
He found some-body - y new.
Oh, let me think, let me think. What shall I
G
C
A♭
do?
Oh no, Oh no.
Oh no no no no no. Re-
Faster (played as)
C
G
C
B♭
C
G
mem-ber walk-ing in the sand.
Re - mem-ber Walk-ing hand in

C Bb C G
hand. Re - mem - ber the night was so ex -
C Bb C G
cit - ing. Re - mem - ber his smile was so in -
C Bb C G C Bb
vit - ing. Re - mem - ber then he touched my cheek. Re -
C G C Bb G
mem - ber with his fin - ger - tips. Re - mem - ber soft - ly,

Tempo 1
C
G
Cm
B♭
soft - ly we met with a kiss.
What ev - er hap - pened to
A♭
Gm
Fm
that boy that I once knew,
the boy that said he'd be
G
Cm
B♭
true?
Oh, what - ev - er hap - pened to
A♭
Gm
Fm
that night I gave it to you?
What will I do with it
What would you do with it

G
Cm
B♭
A♭
Gm
now?
now?
G
Cm
B♭
A♭
Fm
G
C
A♭
Repeat and Fade
Oh no, oh no. Oh no no no no. Re -

LEADER OF THE PACK

Words and Music by GEORGE MORTON,
JEFF BARRY and ELLIE GREENWICH

G7
C
That's when I fell for the lead - er of the pack.
C
My folks were al - ways put - ting him down.
One day my dad said find some - one new.
I felt so help - less, what could I do?
3
They said he came from the wrong side of town.
I had to tell my Jim - my we're through.
Re - mem - b'ring all the things we'd been through.
B♭
G
To Coda

F
Em
They told me he was bad,
He stood there and asked me why,
But I know
But all I could
G7
he was sad,
do was cry,
That's why I fell for the lead - er of the
I'm sor - ry I hurt you, the lead - er of the
1 C
2 C
Bm
pack.
pack.
Am
(Spoken:) He sort of smiled and kissed me goodbye,
But the tears were beginning to show as he drove away

D.S. al Coda
on that rainy night. I begged him to go slow, but whether he heard, I'll never know.
CODA
F
In school they all stop and stare, I
Em
G7
can't hide the tears, but I don't care. I'll nev - er for - get
C
him, the lead - er of the pack.

FOOLISH LITTLE GIRL

Words and Music by HOWARD GREENFIELD
and HELEN MILLER

Dm Gm Cm F6 B♭6
her he's dream-ing of, and there's not a sin - gle thing that you can do.
Fm7 B♭ E♭maj7 Cm7 Fm7 B♭
Solo: But I love him.
Group: No you don't, it's just your pride that's hurt.
Group: It's too late to have a change of heart.
E♭maj7 Cm7 Gm7 C Fmaj7 Dm7
Solo: I still love him.
Group: To - mor - row is his wed - ding day, and you'll keep qui - et if you're smart.
Gm7 F
Group: If you got him back a - gain, you'd go right out and do him hurt.

Dm Gm Dm Gm Cm F6
3fr
Bb Dm Gm Dm Gm
Cm F6 Bb Dm Gm
You fool - ish lit - tle girl,
Dm Gm Cm F6 Bb6
fick-le lit-tle girl, you did-n't want him when he want-ed you. He's

Dm Gm Dm Gm
found an - oth - er love; it's her he's dream - ing of, and there's
Cm F6 B♭6
not a sin - gle thing that you can do. Just for -
(But I love him.)
Cm F6 B♭6 Cm F6
get him 'cause he don't be - long to you. It's too late, he's found some-bod - y
(I still love him.)
B♭6 Cm F6
Repeat and Fade
Optional Ending
new. There's not a sin - gle thing that you can do.
(Oh I love him.)

WILL YOU LOVE ME TOMORROW
(Will You Still Love Me Tomorrow)

Words and Music by GERRY GOFFIN
and CAROLE KING

Eb(add9) Eb Bb/C Cm Fm7/Bb
3 fr
You give your love so sweet - ly.
or just a mo - ment's pleas - ure?
is love I can be sure of.
Bb7 Gsus G7
To - night, the light of love
Can I be - lieve the mag -
So tell me now and I
Cm Bb Cm/Bb Ab(add9)
is in your eyes. But will you
- ic of your sigh? Will you still
won't ask a - gain. Will you still
Bbsus Bb Eb(add9) Eb
To Coda
1
Bb/C Cm
love me to - mor - row, to -
love me to - mor - row?
love me to - mor - row,

A♭maj7
A♭6
3fr
B♭sus
B♭
2
mor - row? _
cresc.
A♭
4fr
Gm
3fr
To - night with words _ un - spok - en ___
mf
A♭
4fr
A♭/B♭
you say that I'm ______ the on - ly one. _
E♭
3fr
B♭/E♭
E♭
3fr
B♭/E♭
E♭
3fr
B♭/E♭
A♭
4fr
But will my

Gm
heart be bro - ken when the night
Cm7 Fsus F7 Fm7 Gm7 A♭ Fm7/B♭
D.S. al Coda
meets the morn - ing sun?
dim.
CODA
B♭/C Cm E♭(add9) E♭ B♭/C Cm B♭/C
to - mor - row?
A♭ B♭ A♭ E♭
Will you still love me to - mor - row?
rit.

WE ARE FAMILY

Words and Music by NILE RODGERS
and BERNARD EDWARDS

D9 A Em7 D9
can see we're to-geth - er as we walk on by.
A Em7 D9
And we flock just like birds of a feath -
A Em7 D9 A Em7
- er. I won't tell no lie. All of the peo -
D9 A Em7 D9
- ple a - round us, they say, "Can they be that close?"

A
Em7
D9
A
Em7
Just let me state for the rec - ord:
We're giv - ing love in a fam -
D9
A7
G(add9)
D
- 'ly dose.
We are fam - i - ly.
F/G
A7
G(add9)
I got all my sis - ters with me.
We are fam - i - ly.
D
F/G
Get up, ev - 'ry - bod - y and sing.

A
Em7
D9
A
Em7
Liv - ing life is fun, and we've just be - gun to get our share _ of this world's
D9
A
Em7
D9
de - lights. _ High hopes we have _ for the fu -
A
Em7
D9
A
Em7
- ture. And our goal's in sight. No, we don't get de - pressed. _
D9
A
Em7
D9
_ Here's what we call _ our _ gold - en rule:

A
Em7
D9
A
Em7
Have faith in you and the things you do. You won't go wrong. This is our fam - 'ly jew - el.
D9
A7
G(add9)
D
We are fam - i - ly.
F/G
A7
G(add9)
I got all my sis - ters with me. We are fam - i - ly.
Repeat and Fade
D
F/G
A7
Get up, ev - 'ry - bod - y, and sing.

STOP

Words and Music by ANDY WATKINS,
PAUL WILSON and SPICE GIRLS

Am7
G
I run a mile. Can't win, you're al - ways right be - hind me.
ba, da, ba, ba. Ba, da, ba, stay that way for - ev - er.
C
B♭
Am7
G
And we know that you could go and find some oth - er. Take or leave it, I just
And we know that you could go and find some oth - er. Take or leave it 'cause we've
C
B♭
don't e - ven both - er. Caught in a craze, it's just a phase,
al - ways got each oth - er. You know who you are, and yes, you're gon - na break down.
Am7
G
Dm
or will this be a - round for - ev - er?
You've crossed the line, so you're gon - na have to turn a - round.
Don't you know it's go - ing

F Em Dm
F Em Dm7
too fast. Rac - ing so hard, you know it won't last.
Em7 Fmaj7 G
Don't you know? Why can't you see? Slow it down, read the sign. Say you know
C B♭
just where you go - ing. Stop right now. Thank you ver - y much. I
Am7 G C B♭
need some - bod - y with a hu - man touch. Hey, you, al -

Am7
G
- ways on the run, got - ta slow it down, ba - by. Got - ta have some fun.
N.C.
C
B♭/C
Got - ta keep it down, hon - ey, lay it back on the line 'cause I don't
F/C
B♭/C
C
B♭/C
care a - bout the mon - ey. Don't be wast - ing my time. You need less speed.

F/C
G
Get off my case. You got-ta slow it down, ba-by. Just get out of my face.
C
B♭
Am7
G
Stop right now. Thank you ver-y much. I need some-bod-y with a
Lead vocal ad lib. 3rd time
hu-man touch. Hey, you, al-ways on the run, got-ta
slow it down, ba-by. Got-ta have some fun.
1,2
3
have some fun.

SAY YOU'LL BE THERE

Words and Music by ELLIOT KENNEDY
and SPICE GIRLS

Am7
D9
4fr
(1.) Last time that we had this con - ver - sa - tion,
(2.) And now you tell me that you're fall - ing in love. Well, I
(D.S.) If you put two and two to - geth - er, you will
Fmaj7
C
I de - cid - ed we should be friends, hey,
nev - er ev - er thought that would be, hey.
see what our friend - ship is for, oh.
Am7
D9
4fr
but now, we're go - ing 'round in cir - cles. Tell me,
This time you got - ta take it eas - y, throw - ing
If you can work this e - qua - tion, then I'll

Fmaj7
1
C
will this dé - jà vu nev - er end, oh?
far too much e - mo - tions at me.
guess I'll have to show you the door.
2, 3
C
Bb/C
But an - y fool can see they're fall -
There is no need to say you love
Fmaj7
Ab/Bb
G9sus
3 fr
- ing. I got - ta make you un - der - stand.
me. It would be bet - ter left un - said.
Am7
D9
4 fr
I'm giv - ing you ev - 'ry - thing, all that joy

Fm6
C
can bring. This I swear.
(1.) I'll give you ev - 'ry - thing.
(2.) Yes, I swear.
Am7
D9
4fr
And all that I want from you is a prom -
To Coda
Fm6
C
- ise you will be there. Say you will be there,
Am
D
Am
yeah. Ow. Say you will be there.

D
D.S. al Coda
(take 2nd ending)
Won't you sing it with me?
CODA
C
Yeah, I
Am7
D9
4fr
Fmaj7
1
C
want you.
Instrumental solo
Vocal 1st time only
2
C
B♭/C
Fmaj7
Solo ends
An - y fool can see they're fall - ing.
I got-ta
A♭/B♭
G9sus
3fr
make you un - der - stand.
I'll

N.C.
give you ev - 'ry-thing, on this I swear, just prom - ise you'll al - ways be there.
Am7
D9
4 fr
I'm giv - ing you ev - 'ry - thing, all that joy
Lead vocal ad lib.
Fm6
C
Am7
can bring. This I swear. And all that I want
D9
4 fr
Fm6
C
Repeat and Fade
from you is a prom - ise you will be there.

TOO MUCH

Words and Music by ANDY WATKINS,
PAUL WILSON and SPICE GIRLS

F+
Dmaj7
G7
need a friend. Road to no-where, twist and turns, but will this nev-er
built to last, S'late I fear, I guess we're run-ning out of time too fast.
Bm
E
end. Well, my dear, you'll know that he pleas - es me. But
Yes, my dear, you know he soothes me. There's
Dmaj7
C#
A
short time so-lu-tion ain't no res-o-lu-tion. There ain't no re-lease from me.
no com-pli-ca-tion, there's no ex-pla-na-tion, it's just a groove in me.
Too much of some-thing is
F+
Dmaj7
G7
bad e-nough, but some-thing's com-ing o-ver me to make me won-der if

A
F+
Dmaj7
too much of noth - ing is just as tough. I need to know the way to feel to
1
G7
2
G7
Bm
keep me sat - is - fied. keep me sat - is - fied. Well, par - don, no, don't you
C♯m
4fr
Gmaj7
F♯(♯5,♯9)
3fr
A
un - der - stand, I want a man not a boy who thinks he can.
F+
Dmaj7
G7
A
Boy who thinks he can.
Too much of some-thing is

F+
Dmaj7
G7
bad e - nough, but some-thing's com - ing o - ver me to make me won - der if
A
F+
Dmaj7
too much of noth - ing is just as tough. I need to know the way to feel to
G7
A
F+
keep me sat - is - fied.
Too much of noth-ing. Some-bod-y may give me a try.
Dmaj7
G7
Repeat and Fade
Opt. Ending
A
Too much of some-thing, you're caught up in liv - ing a lie.

COME SEE ABOUT ME

Words and Music by LAMONT DOZIER,
BRIAN HOLLAND and EDWARD HOLLAND

D Em/A D Em/D D
tears,) but tears won't wash a - way the fear that you're
find un - til you come back and be mine. No
Em/G Bm
nev - er ev - er gon - na re - turn to ease the
mat - ter what you do or say, I'm
arms you may be out of reach, but my
Em/G Bm
fire that with - in me burns. It keeps me
gon - na love you an - y - way, keep on
heart says you're here to keep. It keeps me
Em F♯m G Em F♯m
cry - ing, ba - by, for you, keeps me sigh - ing, ba - by, for
cry - ing, ba - by, for you. I'm gon - na keep sigh - ing, ba - by, for
cry - ing, ba - by, for you, keep on cry - ing, ba - by, for

G
Gm
3fr
G
you. So won't you hur - ry? Come on, boy,
you. So come on, hur - ry. Come on and see a - bout
you. So won't you hur - ry? Come on, boy,
D
Em/D
D
Em/D
D
Em/D
To Coda
(Harmony on D.S. only)
me. See a - bout you, ba - by.
(Come see a - bout me.) (Come see a - bout
1
D
Em/B
Em/A
D
Em/D
D
Em/A
I've giv - en up my friends just (for you.) My friends have gone and
me.)
D
Em/D
D
Em/A
D
2
D
Em/D
you have too. No peace me.)

Em/G D Em/G
D Em/D D Em/D
Some - times up,
D Em/D D Em/D D Em/D
some - times down,
my life's so un -
D Em/D D Em/A D Em/D
cer - tain
with you not a - round.

D
D.S. al Coda
From my
CODA
D Em/D
You know I'm so lone -
me.)
D Em/D D Em/D D Em/D
(Fade out)
- ly.
(Come see a - bout me.)
I love you on - ly.
(Come see a - bout
D Em/D D Em/D
See a - bout you, ba - by.
me.)
(Come see a - bout
D Em/D D Em/D D
Hur - ry, hur - ry.
me.)
(Come see a - bout me.)

STOP! IN THE NAME OF LOVE

Words and Music by LAMONT DOZIER,
BRIAN HOLLAND and EDWARD HOLLAND

Cmaj7
Gm
3fr
3
Ba - by, ba - by, I'm a - ware _ of where you go each time you
A7
F
G
leave my door. _ I watch you walk down the street, _
F
G
C
know - ing your oth - er love you'll meet. _
But this time _ be - fore you
But this time _ be - fore you
G/B
F
run to her, leav - ing me a - lone _ and hurt, ___
leave my arms and rush off to ___ her charms, _
(Think it

C F/C C
af - ter I've been good to you,
have - n't I been good to you?
o - ver.) (Think it
F/C C Am
af - ter I've been sweet - to you,
have - n't I been sweet - to you?
o - ver.)
Stop! In the
G/B F G
name of love, be - fore you break my heart.
Am G/B F
To Coda
Stop! In the name of love, be - fore you

G
C
F/C
C
break my heart. Think it o - ver. Think it
F/C
C
o - ver.
I've known of your,
I've tried so hard,
Cmaj7
Gm
3fr
A7
your se - clud - ed nights, I've e - ven seen her may - be once or twice.
hard to be pa - tient, hop - ing you'd stop this in - fat - u - a - tion.
F
G
But is her sweet ex - pres - sion
But each time you are to - geth - er,

F
1
G
worth more than my love and af - fec - tion?
I'm so a - fraid of
2
G
D.S. al Coda
los - ing you for - ev - er.
CODA
G
Am
break my heart. Stop! In the
G/B
F
Repeat and Fade
name of love, be - fore you break my heart.
Optional Ending
G
break my heart. Think it
C
F/C
C
F/C
C
o - ver. Think it o - ver.

MY WORLD IS EMPTY WITHOUT YOU

Words and Music by EDWARD HOLLAND,
LAMONT DOZIER and BRIAN HOLLAND

Moderately bright, with a beat

F#m
D
And as I go my way a - lone,
From this old world I try to hide
A/C#
Em
my face,
I find it hard
but from this lone -
Bm/D
A7♭9
6fr
A
for me to car - ry on.
- li - ness there's no hid - ing place.
D
A/C#
I need your strength, I need your ten - der touch,
In - side this cold and emp - ty house I dwell,

Em
I need the love, my dear, I
in dark-ness with mem - o - ries I
Bm
A7
miss so much.
know so well.
Bm
G
A/C♯
I need love now more

Am/C
F
than be - fore,
I can hard -
Dm
A
- ly car - ry on an - y - more.
Bm
G
My world is emp - ty with - out you, babe,
Bm
with - out you, babe,

G
F♯m
with - out
you, _
babe. _
D
A/C♯
My
mind and
soul ___
have
felt ___
like
this ___
Em
since
love
be - tween __
us ______
no
Bm/D
A7♭9
A
more
ex - ists. _____

D
A/C#
And each time that dark - ness falls,
Em
it finds me a - lone with
Bm
A7
Bm
these four walls.
My world is emp -
G
Repeat and Fade
- ty with - out you, babe.

YOU CAN'T HURRY LOVE

Words and Music by EDWARD HOLLAND,
LAMONT DOZIER and BRIAN HOLLAND

Dm Gm E♭ F7 B♭
"Love don't come eas - y. It's a game of give and take. You can't hur - ry love. No, you
"Love don't come eas - y. It's a game of give and take." How long must I wait, how much
E♭ B♭ Dm Gm E♭ F7
just have to wait. You got - ta trust, give it time, no mat - ter how long it takes." But
more can I take be - fore lone - li - ness will cause my heart, heart to break? No,
Dm Gm
how man - y heart - aches must I stand be - fore I find a love to let me
I can't bear to live my life a - lone. I grow im - pa - tient for a love to
E♭6
live a - gain? Right now the on - ly thing that keeps me hang - ing on, when I
call my own, but when I feel that I, I can't go on, these

F
Dm/F
E♭/F
F7
B♭
feel my strength, yeah, it's al-most gone, I re-mem-ber ma - ma said, "Can't hur - ry love. No, you
pre-cious words keeps me hang-ing on; I re-mem-ber ma - ma said, can't hur - ry love. No, you
E♭
3 fr
B♭
Dm
Gm
1
F7
just have to wait." She said, "Love don't come eas - y, it's a game of give and take. You
just have to wait." She said, "Trust, give it time, no
2
mat - ter how long it takes."
No love, love don't come
Gm7
eas - y, but I keep on wait - ing, an - tic - i - pat - ing for that

B♭ E♭ B♭ Dm Gm7
3fr 3fr
soft voice to talk to me at night, for some ten-der arms to
E♭ F7 B♭ E♭ B♭
3fr 3fr
hold me tight. I keep wait-ing, I keep on wait - ing, but it ain't
Dm Gm E♭ F7 B♭
3fr 3fr
eas - y, it ain't eas - y when ma - ma said, "You can't hur - ry love. No, you
E♭ B♭ Dm Gm E♭ F7
3fr 3fr 3fr
Repeat and Fade
just have to wait." She said,
"Trust, give it time, no mat - ter how long it takes."
"Love don't come eas - y, it's a game of give and take."
You

YOU KEEP ME HANGIN' ON

Words and Music by EDWARD HOLLAND,
LAMONT DOZIER and BRIAN HOLLAND

This edition has been transposed up one half-step from the original recording to be more playable.

G/D
F
Am/E
A
me hang - in' on.
You don't real - ly need
Now you don't real - ly want
G6
G/D
F
Am/E
me, but you keep me hang - in' on.
me, you just keep me hang - in' on.
C7sus
F
Why do you keep a - com - in' a - round, play - in' a - with my heart?
You say, al - though we broke up, you still wan - na be just friends.
C
C7sus
Why don't you get out of my life
But how can we still be friends when

1
F
C
Em/B
G
and let me make a new start? Let me get o -
- ver you the way you've got - ten o - ver me. Hey.
E7
2
F
A
N.C.
see - ing you on - ly breaks my heart a - gain?
(Spoken:) And there ain't nothing I can do about it.
A
G6
(Whoa, oh, oh.) Set me free. Why don't you, babe? (Whoa, oh,

G/D
F
Am/E
A
oh.) Get out my life. Why don't you, ba - by? Set me free. Why don't
G6
G/D
F
Am/E
you, ba - by? Get out my life. Why don't you, ba - by?
C7sus
F
You claim you still care for me, but your heart and soul needs to be free.
C
C7sus
And now that you've got your free - dom, you

F C Em/B G
want to still hold on to me. You don't want me
E7
for your-self, so let me find some-bod - y else. Hey, hey.
A G6 G/D
Why don't you be a man a - bout it and set me free?
F Am/E A G6
Now you don't care a thing a - bout me,

G/D F Am/E A
you're just us - ing me. Go on, get out, get out
G6 G/D F Am/E
of my life and let me sleep at night. Please.
A G6 G/D
'Cause you don't real - ly love me, you just keep me hang - in' on.
F Am/E
Repeat and Fade
A
You don't real - ly need
Optional Ending
A

WHERE DID OUR LOVE GO

Words and Music by BRIAN HOLLAND,
LAMONT DOZIER and EDWARD HOLLAND

G
yearn - ing feel - in' in - side me. Ooh, deep in -
Dm
G
To Coda
side me and it hurts so bad.
F(add9)
C
3
You came in - to my heart (ba - by ba - by) so ten - der -
G
Dm7
ly with a burn - ing love (ba - by ba - by)

G
F
C
that stings like a bee. (ba-by ba-by) Now that I sur-ren-der (ba-by ba-by)
G
Dm7
so help-less-ly, you now want to leave. (ba-by ba-by)
3
G
F(add9)
C
Ooh, you wan-na leave me. (ba-by ba-by) Ooh. (ba-by ba-by) Ba-by, ba-by,
G
Dm7
where did our love go? Ooh, don't you want me?

G7
F(add9)
Don't you want me no more? (ba - by ba - by) Ooh, ba - by.
C
G
Dm7
G
F(add9)
D.C. al Coda
CODA
F(add9)
Be - fore you won my

C
G
heart, (ba-by ba-by) you were a per-fect guy. But now that you
Dm7
G
N.C.
got me, you wan-na leave me be - hind. (ba-by ba-by) Ooh, ba - by.
C
G
Ba - by, ba - by, ba - by, don't leave me. Ooh, please don't
Dm7
G
N.C.
Repeat and Fade
leave me all by my - self. (ba-by ba-by) Ooh.

CREEP

Words and Music by
DALLAS AUSTIN

Fm7
Cm7
Fm7/E♭
Fm7
es - ty, but I know __ he's cheat - ing on me.
but I'm not bug-gin' 'cause I _____ still feel __ the same.
Cm7
Fm7
Cm7
I look him in his eyes, but all he tells me is lies ___ to keep _ me near.
I keep giv - ing lov - ing till the day he push - es me a - way. Nev - er go ___ a - stray.
Fm7/E♭
Fm7
Cm7
Fm7
I'll nev - er leave him down, though I might mess a - round. It's
If he knew the things I did, he could-n't han-dle me.
Cm7
Fm7/E♭
Fm7
Cm7
on - ly 'cause I need some af - fec - tion, oh. _______
And I choose to keep him pro - tect - ed, oh. _______
So I creep, yeah, _____ just
3 fr

Fm7
Cm7
creep - in' on, but I'll know, 'cept no - bod - y is sup - posed _ to know. _
Fm7/E♭
Fm7
Cm7
Fm7
So I creep, yeah, _ 'cause he does-n't know what I do and
Cm7
Fm7/E♭
Fm7
Cm7
no at - ten - tion goes _ to show, _ oh. _ So I creep, yeah, _ just
creep, yeah, _ 'cause
Fm7
Cm7
Fm7/E♭
Fm7
Repeat ad lib. and Fade
creep-in' on, but I'll know, 'cept no-bod-y is sup - posed _ to know, _ So I
he does-n't know what I do, and no at - ten-tion goes _ to show. _ So I

NO SCRUBS

Words and Music by KANDI L. BURRUSS,
TAMEKA COTTLE and KEVIN BRIGGS

Original key: G♯ minor. This edition has been transposed down one half-step to be more playable.

Gm
D7
G5
3fr
what he wants and just sits on his broke ass.
look-in' like trash. Can't get wit' a dead beat ass.
So,
Cm7
Gm
D7
no, I don't want your num-ber. No, I don't wan-na
Gm
Cm7
Gm
D7
give you mine and no, I don't wan-na meet you no-where. No, don't want
G5
Cm7
Gm
D7
none of your time and no, I don't want no scrub. A scrub is a guy that can't

Gm
Cm7
Gm
3 fr
get no love from me, hang - in' out the pas - sen - ger side of his
D7
Gm
Cm7
Gm
best friend's ride, try'n to hol - ler at me. I don't want no scrub. A
D7
Gm
Cm7
scrub is a guy that can't get no love from me, hang - in' out the
Gm
D7
1
Gm
pas - sen - ger side of his best friend's ride, try'n to hol - ler at
A

2
Gm
3fr
Ebmaj9
try'n to hol - ler at me.
If you don't have a car ___ and you're walk - in', oh, yes, _
D7b9
4fr
F/G
___ son, I'm talk - in' to you. If you live at home _ wit' your
Gb
Fm
E7
ma - ma, oh, yes, ___ son, I'm talk - in' to you. If you
Ebmaj7
3fr
D7/F#
have as - sured _ me that you don't show love, oh, yes, son, ___ I'm

Gm7
C7
talk - in' to you. Wan - na get with me with no mon - ey, oh
F9sus
D7/F♯
Cm7
no, I don't want no...
No
Gm
D7
Gm
scrub.
Cm7
Gm
D7
G5
No
scrub.
No, no.

Cm7 Gm D7
1 Gm
No, scrub.
2 G5 Cm7 Gm D7
No, no. No, I don't want no scrub. A scrub is a guy that can't
me.
Gm Cm7 Gm
get no love from me, hang - in' out the pas - sen ger side of his
D7
Repeat and Fade Gm
Optional Ending Gm
best friend's ride, try'n to hol - ler at try'n to hol - ler at me.

UNPRETTY

Words and Music by DALLAS AUSTIN
and TIONNE WATKINS

* *Vocal line is written an octave higher than sung.*

*Vocal line is written as sung.

F/A G C G/B C/G F F/A G
cause of you. I try dif - f'rent ways but it's all the same. At the
C G/D C/B F/A G
end of the day I have my - self to blame. I'm just trip - pin'.
I have my - self to blame. Be - lieve I'm trip - pin'.
C G/B C/G F F/A G
You can buy your hair if it won't grow. You can fix your nose if he says so.
C G/D C/B F/A G
You can buy all the make - up that man can make. But if

C G/B C/G F F/A G
you can't look in - side you, find out who am I, too.
C G/D C/B
Be in the po - si - tion to make me
1
F/A G C G/B C/G
feel so damn un - pret - ty.
F F/A G C G/D C/B F/A G
Yeah, I make you feel un - pret - ty, too.
2
F/A G
feel so damn un - pret - ty.
C G/B C/G
You can buy your hair if it won't grow.

F F/A G C G/D C/B
You can fix your nose if he says so.
You can buy all the make - up the
F/A G C G/B C/G F F/A G
man can make. But if you can't look in - side you, find out who am I, too.
C G/D C/B F/A
To Coda
G C G/B C/G
Be in the po - si - tion to make me feel so damn un - pret - ty.
F F/A G C G/D C/B
I make you feel un - pret - ty, too.

F/A G C G/B C/G
I make you feel un - pret - ty.
F F/A G C G/D C/B
F/A G C G/B C/G F F/A G
Oh. Oh, oh.
C G/D C/B F/A G C G/B C/G F F/A G
Oh. Oh, oh. Oh. Oh, oh.

D.S. al Coda
C
G/D
C/B
F/A
G
Oh.
Oh, oh.
CODA
G/B
C/G
You can buy your hair if it won't grow.
F
You can buy all the make - up that
man can make. But if
you can't look in - side you.
Be in the po - si - tion to make me feel so.
Repeat and Fade
Optional Ending

HOLD ON

Words and Music by CARNI
CHYNNA PHILLIPS and GLEN

F C/F B♭/F C/E
o - pen your heart and your mind, mm.
let - tin' your wor - ries pass you by, ba - by.
Dm F(add9)/A B♭ B♭/C
Is it real-ly fair to feel this way in - side? Woh,
Don't you think it's worth your time to change your mind? No, no,
F B♭/F C/F F
Some day some-bod-y's gon-na make you wan-na turn a-round and say good-bye.
B♭/F C/F F
Un-til then ba - by, are you gon-na let him hold you down and make you cry? Don't you know

B♭/F
C/F
F
To Coda
don't you know things could change? Things-'ll go your way if you hold
B♭
F/A
Gm7
Gm7/C
on for one more day. Can you hold on for one
Gm7
Gm7/C
1
no chord
more day? Things-'ll go your way. Hold on for one more day.
F
C/F
B♭(add9)/F
C/F
F
C/F
B♭(add9)/F

2
no chord
F
C/F
B♭/F
Hold on for one more day.
I know that there is pain, but ya
C/F
F
C/F
B♭/F
hold on for one more day, and ya
break free from the chains.
F
C/F
B♭/F
C/F
Yeah, I know that there is pain, but ya
hold on for one more day, and ya
D.S. al Coda
break free break from the chains.
CODA
B♭
F/A
on for one

Gm7
Gm7/C
F
B♭/F
C/F
F
more day, yeah. Hold on.
B♭/F
C/F
F
B♭/F
Don't you know, things could change?
C/F
F
B♭
F/A
Things could go your way if you hold on for one
Gm7
Gm7/C
F
B♭/F
C/F
F
Repeat ad lib. and Fade
more day, if you hold on. Can you hold on?

IMPULSIVE

Words and Music by STEVE KIPNER
and CLIF MAGNESS

E
E/G♯
C♯m
the way it's sup - posed to be. I nev - er im -
G♯m
Bm
A
ag - ined you could blow my theo - ry a - part.
E/G♯
A
E/G♯
F♯m
E/G♯
A
Bsus
But now you're run - ing a - way with my heart
no chord
I don't wan - na think a -

E E/G♯ A E E/G♯
bout it, don't wan-na think clear, don't an - a - lyze what I'm
A A/B C♯m B/D♯ E
do - ing here. Wan-na be im - pul - sive, reck - less, and
A Bsus E Esus
lose my - self in your kiss.
E Esus

E
E/G♯
A
Ar - rows through hearts
drawn on a
Bsus
B
E
E/G♯
mis - ty win - dow.
You're tak - ing me home in the rain.
F♯m7
E/G♯
F♯m
E
Bsus
My heart is beat - ing. Don't say no. My
F♯m
E
Bsus
head keeps say - ing take it slow.

Bsus
no chord
E
E/G#
I don't wan - na think a - bout it, don't wan - na
A
E
E/G#
A
Bsus
think clear, don't an - a - lyze what I'm do - ing here. Wan - na be im -
C#m
B/D#
E
A
pul - sive, reck - less, and lose my - self in your
Bsus
E
E/G#
A
kiss. You're giv - ing me a feel - ing it's a sud - den rush. Act - ing on the

E
E/G#
A
mo - ment, it's spon - ta - ne - ous. Wo wo
F#m
E/G#
A
Bsus
oh. This is not like me to
F#m7
E/G#
A
Bsus
fol - low my heart so eas - i - ly.
E7sus

E
I am reck - less, im - pul - sive.
D
C#m
I nev - er im -
G#m
Bm
A
ag - ined you could blow my theo - ry a - part. But
F#m
E
Bsus
now you're run - ning a - way with my heart,

E
Esus
E
Esus
my heart.
E
E/G♯
I don't wan - na think a - bout it, don't wan - na
feel - ing. It's a
A
E
E/G♯
think clear, don't an - a - lyze what I'm
sud - den rush. Act - ing on the mo ment, it's spon -
A
A/B
C♯m
B/D♯
E
do - ing here.
ta - ne - ous.
Wan - na be im - pul - sive, reck - less, and

A
1
Bsus
lose my - self in your kiss. You're giv - in' me a
2
Bsus
E
E/G#
A
kiss. Woh. Im - pul - sive, I wan - na be
Instrumental on repeat
E
E/G#
A
A/B
C#m
im - pul - sive. I'm gon - na be im - pul - sive,
B/D#
E
A
A/B
Repeat ad lib. and Fade
reck - less, and lose my - self, lose my - self.

Contemporary Classics

Your favorite songs for piano, voice and guitar.

The Definitive Rock 'n' Roll Collection

A classic collection of the best songs from the early rock 'n' roll years – 1955-1966. 97 songs, including: Barbara Ann • Chantilly Lace • Dream Lover • Duke of Earl • Earth Angel • Great Balls of Fire • Louie, Louie • Rock Around the Clock • Ruby Baby • Runaway • (Seven Little Girls) Sitting in the Back Seat • Stay • Surfin' U.S.A. • Wild Thing • Woolly Bully • and more.

00490195..$27.95

The Big Book of Rock

78 of rock's biggest hits, including: Addicted to Love • American Pie • Born to Be Wild • Cold As Ice • Dust in the Wind • Free Bird • Goodbye Yellow Brick Road • Groovin' • Hey Jude • I Love Rock 'N' Roll • Lay Down Sally • Layla • Livin' on a Prayer • Louie Louie • Maggie May • Me and Bobby McGee • Monday, Monday • Owner of a Lonely Heart • Shout • Walk This Way • We Didn't Start the Fire • You Really Got Me • and more.

00311566..$19.95

Big Book of Movie Music

Features 73 classic songs from 72 movies: Beauty and the Beast • Change the World • Eye of the Tiger • I Finally Found Someone • The John Dunbar Theme • Somewhere in Time • Stayin' Alive • Take My Breath Away • Unchained Melody • The Way You Look Tonight • You've Got a Friend in Me • Zorro's Theme • more.

00311582..$19.95

The Best Rock Songs Ever

70 of the best rock songs from yesterday and today, including: All Day and All of the Night • All Shook Up • Ballroom Blitz • Bennie and the Jets • Blue Suede Shoes • Born to Be Wild • Boys Are Back in Town • Every Breath You Take • Faith • Free Bird • Hey Jude • I Still Haven't Found What I'm Looking For • Livin' on a Prayer • Lola • Louie Louie • Maggie May • Money • (She's) Some Kind of Wonderful • Takin' Care of Business • Walk This Way • We Didn't Start the Fire • We Got the Beat • Wild Thing • more!

00490424..$17.95

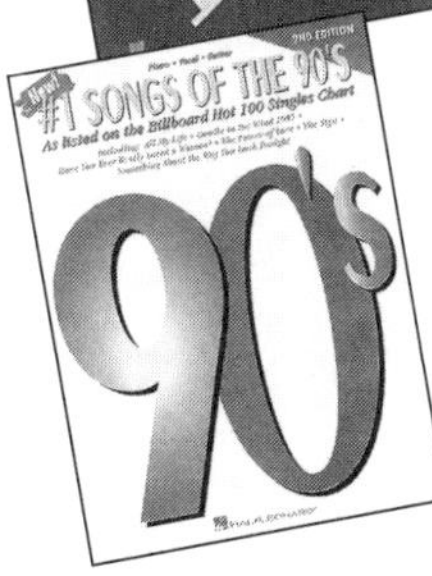

#1 Songs of the '90s

21 top hits as listed on the *Billboard* Hot 100 Singles Chart. Songs include: All My Life • Candle in the Wind 1997 • The Power of Love • The Sign • and more.

00310018..$12.95

Motown Anthology

This songbook commemorates Motown's 40th Anniversary with 68 songs, background information on this famous record label, and lots of photos. Songs include: ABC • Baby Love • Ben • Dancing in the Street • Easy • For Once in My Life • My Girl • Shop Around • The Tracks of My Tears • War • What's Going On • You Can't Hurry Love • and many more.

00310367..$19.95

"My Heart Will Go On (Love Theme from 'Titanic')" & 23 More Songs from Today's Hit Movies

Includes these megahits: (I Love You) For Sentimental Reasons (*As Good As It Gets*) • You Must Love Me (*Evita*) • Miss Misery (*Good Will Hunting*) • You Sexy Thing (*The Full Monty*) • I Say a Little Prayer (*My Best Friend's Wedding*) • and more.

00310417..$10.95

Women of Modern Rock

25 songs from contemporary chanteuses, including: As I Lay Me Down • Connection • Feed the Tree • Galileo • Here and Now • Look What Love Has Done • Love Sneakin' Up on You • Walking on Broken Glass • You Oughta Know • Zombie • and more.

00310093..$14.95

Jock Rock Hits

32 stadium-shaking favorites, including: Another One Bites the Dust • The Boys Are Back in Town • Freeze-Frame • Gonna Make You Sweat (Everybody Dance Now) • I Got You (I Feel Good) • Na Na Hey Hey Kiss Him Goodbye • Rock & Roll – Part II (The Hey Song) • Shout • Tequila • We Are the Champions • We Will Rock You • Whoomp! (There It Is) • Wild Thing • and more.

00310105..$14.95

Rock Ballads

31 sentimental favorites, including: All for Love • Bed of Roses • Dust in the Wind • Everybody Hurts • Right Here Waiting • Tears in Heaven • and more.

00311673..$14.95

FOR MORE INFORMATION, SEE YOUR LOCAL MUSIC DEALER,
OR WRITE TO:

HAL•LEONARD™ CORPORATION

7777 W. BLUEMOUND RD. P.O. BOX 13819 MILWAUKEE, WI 53213

Visit Hal Leonard Online at www.halleonard.com

Prices, contents & availability subject to change without notice.